# Living the Message of the New Testament

# Living the Message of the New Testament

Michael Pennock

AVE MARIA PRESS
NOTRE DAME, INDIANA 46556

*Nihil Obstat:* The Reverend Edward E. Mehok, Ph.D.
Censor Deputatus

*Imprimatur:* The Most Reverend Anthony M. Pilla, D.D., M.A.
Bishop of Cleveland

Given at Cleveland, Ohio on 1 October 1991

Excerpts from THE DOCUMENTS OF VATICAN II, Abbott-Gallagher edition, reprinted with permission of America Press, Inc., 106 West 56th Street, New York, NY 10019. © 1966 All Rights Reserved.

Excerpts from THE NEW JERUSALEM BIBLE, copyright © 1985 by Darton, Longman & Todd, Ltd. and Doubleday & Company, Inc. Reprinted by permission of the publisher.

---

© 1992 by Ave Maria Press, Notre Dame, IN 46556

All rights reserved. No part of this book may be used or reproduced in any manner whatsoever without written permission, except in the case of reprints in the context of reviews.

International Standard Book Number: 0-87793-469-X

Library of Congress Catalog Card Number: 91-77474

Cover and text design by Katherine Robinson Coleman

Photography:

Art Resource 37, 48, 79, 138, 141, 150, 166, 172, 192; Gail Denham 8, 65; Editorial Development Association 61, 72-73, 142 (bottom), 178-179, 181; Don Franklin Photography 157; Luke Golobitsh 26 (top); Janet Newport 137; Marilyn Nolt 105, 123; Richard Nowitz cover, 11, 12-13, 28, 34, 35, 40, 45, 53, 68, 80, 81, 86, 112-113, 139, 165, 191; Gene Plaisted 18, 23, 26 (bottom), 102, 108, 116, 128, 142 (top), 147, 155, 159, 183, 185, 195, 199; Zev Radovan 15, 56, 83; Religious News Service 22, 62, 70-71, 82, 140; Vernon Sigl 132-133; Vada Snider 76; Justin Soleta 98-99, 202; Strix Pix 93; Sunrise/Trinity 95; Renauld Thomas 107; Jim West 66, 130; Jim Whitmer 97.

Printed and bound in the United States of America.

I dedicate this book to my wife Carol with love.

# Contents

*chapter* 1

# Introducing the New Testament

"Did not our hearts burn within us as he talked to us on the road and explained the scriptures to us?"

— Luke 24:32

**In This Chapter**

**We will look at:**

- **relationship between the Old and New Testaments**
- **how the Christian scriptures were formed**
- **background helps for reading the New Testament**

You are about to begin an exciting journey, a study of the New Testament. As a young adult, you have so many concerns pressing in on you — decisions about your future, friends to make and keep, relating to members of the opposite sex, figuring out how you will use your talents to make a living. The list is endless. In the midst of all this, you might wonder how reading the New Testament can be exciting.

Christians through the centuries have found in their sacred scriptures the key to life's meaning. Countless millions have discovered Jesus in the Bible. This meeting with the Lord brings about the same experience as that of the two disciples who met Jesus on the road to Emmaus after the resurrection: Their hearts burned with love.

William Arthur Ward, a contemporary inspirational writer, has written:

> It is not enough to own a Bible; we must read it.
> It is not enough to read it; we must let it speak to us.
> It is not enough to let it speak to us; we must believe it.
> It is not enough to believe it; we must live it.

How can we judge whether the Bible will make a real difference in our lives? We must follow the advice given. Read the Bible. Let it speak to your heart. Believe the good news you read. Put into practice what you learn and experience.

This text will introduce you to the books of the New Testament. Because of space and time limitations, we will focus primarily on the gospels, the Acts of the Apostles, and key letters of St. Paul. Throughout our study, we will see how the New Testament gives meaning to our lives today.

## New Testament Themes

The Christian scriptures contain life-giving themes that make them good news for our day and all ages. Here are some of the most important themes you will discover. Circle the number that reflects your present attitude to each of these summary statements: **5** — is very meaningful to me; **1** — doesn't affect me.

■ *discuss* ■

**Have Christians done a good job in spreading the message contained in these themes? Explain.**

1. God loves you beyond what you can imagine. You are precious in God's eyes.

   5 4 3 2 1

2. Jesus Christ, God's Son, is your Lord, Savior, and friend.

   5 4 3 2 1

3. The Lord invites you to new life. But first you must *repent*, that is, you must turn from anything that keeps you from being a loving person.

   5 4 3 2 1

4. The Father and the Son have given you the Holy Spirit. The Spirit has endowed you with many gifts.

   5 4 3 2 1

5. You can find the Lord in your Christian brothers and sisters, the church. The church is your spiritual family.

   5 4 3 2 1

6. God expects wonderful things from you. God especially wants you to meet the needs of those who are hurting.

   5 4 3 2 1

■ *journal* ■

Below are New Testament passages that correspond to the themes summarized above. Please read the passage and match it with the theme it illustrates. Then briefly summarize what the passage is about.

Finally, write a short paragraph discussing what one of these passages means to you.

A. Matthew 25:31–46
B. James 1:16–27
C. Luke 15:1–7
D. 1 Corinthians 13
E. John 15:13–17
F. Matthew 18:20

## Relationship Between the Old and New Testaments

For the disciples of Jesus, living in the first century, "the scriptures" were the Hebrew scriptures, what we traditionally called the Old Testament. It took the disciples seventy years, beginning around the year 50, to develop their own sacred writings, which we call the New Testament.

The New Testament contains twenty-seven books in all, the most important of which are the four gospels. These gospels — Matthew, Mark, Luke, and John — testify to God's saving deeds in his Son, Jesus the Messiah. The Acts of the Apostles describes the Spirit-led growth of the early church. The thirteen letters traditionally ascribed to St. Paul tell us about the life of the early church and give directions for Christian living. The New Testament also includes other letters — Hebrews, Jude, Peter, James, and John — and a highly symbolic work called the Apocalypse or the Book of Revelation.

*Covenant in the Hebrew Scriptures.* The Hebrew word for covenant can be translated as testament. When Christians called their sacred scriptures the *New* Testament, they were saying that God established a new covenant with his people in Jesus Christ. The theme of testament or covenant fills the pages of the Hebrew scriptures. From its opening book, Genesis, the Hebrew scriptures reveal a God involved in the lives of his creatures. This God created human beings (Adam and Eve) and kept them alive even though they turned their backs on him. God renewed this covenant of life with Noah at the time of the flood.

God then formed a special people, beginning with a formal covenant with Abraham (c. 1900 B.C.) through whom God would bless all nations. God's covenant with the Chosen People was a special kind of contract: God would continually bless and be faithful to his people; for their part, they

were to obey and worship the one true God. The Hebrew word that describes God's fidelity to the covenant is *hesed,* which is translated "loving-kindness."

## journal

Review some key passages from the Hebrew scriptures that tell us of God's covenant with the Chosen People and its requirements. Read one passage from each of the categories below and summarize them in your journal.

*Covenant with Abraham:* Gn 12; 15; 19; 21–22

*Moses and Exodus:* Ex 1—6:13; 7—11; 12:21–41; 13:17–22; 14; 15:19–27; 19—20; 24; 32—34:9

*Into the Promised Land:* Jos 3—4

*David:* 1 Sm 16—19; 2 Sm 11—12

*Prophets remind Jews to be faithful to the covenant:* Hos 2:4—3:5; Am 2:6–16; Jer 31:31–34

*Hope kept alive in captivity:* Is 40:1–11

The Hebrew scriptures reveal God's loving-kindness throughout salvation history. Most notably, God rescued the Hebrews from slavery in Egypt (the Exodus) and renewed his covenant with Moses on Mount Sinai (c. 1300 B.C.). There he promised the Hebrews a land; in return the people were to live the Law as a concrete demonstration of their love. He also revealed his name as *Yahweh,* which means "I am who am."

For forty years God's people wandered the desert as a preparation for inheriting the Promised Land. Eventually, they entered Palestine and formed a strong nation under King David (c. 1000–961 B.C.), who symbolized for the Jews the hope that one day Yahweh would send a Messiah. This future king would rule with true justice and firmly establish God's peace throughout the world.

The Hebrew scriptures depict the people's infidelity to the Law and Yahweh. They sinned and fell into worship of false gods. Their dissolute living led to the disintegration of a united kingdom. The northern kingdom of Israel fell to Assyria in 722 B.C., and the southern kingdom of Judah was overrun by the Babylonians in 587 B.C. Nearly all the people were taken prisoner and exiled in Babylon. The prophet Jeremiah warned against infidelity to the covenant. Other prophets railed against oppression of the poor, but their words fell on deaf ears.

Captivity in Babylon (587–537 B.C.) was a low point in this period of Jewish history, but even in exile Yahweh did not abandon his people. Prophets such as the author of Second Isaiah kept alive the hope of an eventual return to their own land. He also promised that God would send a Servant-Messiah who would save the people. When Persia captured Babylon, the Jews were allowed to return to Israel. There they could once again worship Yahweh in the Temple in Jerusalem. Ezra, Nehemiah, and others reorganized the Jewish religion and continually reminded the people of God's covenant.

Even after the return from exile, the people still needed reminders of God's fidelity because foreign powers — Persians, Greeks, Seleucids, and finally the Romans — ruled them in turn. During the rule of the Romans, Jesus was born. Through him and in him Yahweh showed once and for all that he was faithful to his word. This new covenant was to be sealed in the blood of his Son.

*Jesus Is the New Covenant.* Jesus fulfilled the Law by giving a new law of love that requires us to look to our interior motives as well as our external behavior. He taught that God's covenant love extends not only to the Chosen People but to all people everywhere.

Jesus also fulfilled the prophets. First, he was himself the perfect prophet who spoke for God because he was God's own Son. His words and his actions showed that God was actively present in the world, saving, redeeming, and healing people. Jesus proclaimed the coming of God's reign and showed in his words and actions that the reign of God was powerfully alive in the world.

Second, Jesus' life and ministry also reveal him as the fulfillment of the prophet's hope for a Servant-Messiah. His message of complete trust in God, his healing of the sick, and his compassion toward sinners bring to completion the witness of the prophets of the first covenant.

Finally, Jesus was God's new covenant. This covenant was signed and sealed in the blood he shed on the cross. His resurrection is the ultimate expression of God's fidelity to the covenant. When the Son of God freely gave up his life for our salvation, he initiated a new relationship with all of humanity, not just with the people of Israel. This new relationship requires faith in Jesus as God's Son, our Savior, Lord, and Messiah.

The Christian scriptures continue and fulfill the Hebrew scriptures; they do not contradict them. The New Testament reveals that God has extended his loving-kindness and his salvation to all people. Jesus is the new covenant. The New Testament books tell Jesus' story and what our relationship to him should be.

## How the Christian Scriptures Were Formed

Scripture scholars have concluded that the following three stages were involved in the formation of the Christian scriptures:

*Stage 1: The Historical Jesus:* 6 B.C.-A.D. 30
Jesus is born in 6 B.C. and lives a normal Jewish life until he comes on the public scene in the year 28.

> *Public life (28–30):* Jesus teaches, heals, and proclaims God's reign. He forms a group of apostles to carry on his work. Pontius Pilate has him crucified in April of 30.

*Stage 2: Oral Tradition:* 30–50
The disciples live their life in light of the resurrection of Jesus. They reflect on his meaning. They *preach, teach,* and *worship* in his name.

They begin to assemble collections of Jesus material — for example, miracle stories, parables, the passion narrative. They first preach throughout Palestine, but later move out to the whole Mediterranean world. Paul writes his first letter around 51.

*Stage 3: Written Letters and Gospels*
50s and 60s: Pauline epistles
65–100: gospels
90–110: Revelation and other "apostolic" writings

*Stage 1: The Historical Jesus.* Jesus was born in Bethlehem during the reign of Herod the Great, probably around 6 B.C.

His mother was Mary and his step-father was Joseph. He came from Nazareth, in the region of Galilee, an area looked down on by the people of Jerusalem. His contemporaries knew him as Jesus the carpenter, or Jesus the son of Joseph (Mark's gospel calls him the son of Mary). He lived the life of a pious Jew. He worshipped on the Sabbath, recited his daily prayers, celebrated the great religious feasts, and kept the precepts of the Law.

The "synagogue-church" in Nazareth where Jesus preached.

Jesus began his public ministry in Galilee, probably in the year 28. He preached a message of repentance and faith in the coming of God's reign. He gathered a group of followers or disciples who observed his life, heard his teaching, and witnessed his miracles.

Many people believed that Jesus was a prophet or spokesperson for God. Yet, some of Jesus' own acquaintances and relatives from Nazareth rejected him:

> He went home again, and once more such a crowd collected that they could not even have a meal. When his relations heard of this, they set out to take charge of him; they said, "He is out of his mind" (Mk 3:20–21).

His teaching was forceful. For example, he often introduced his words with "I say to you," in contrast to his contemporaries who typically quoted other teachers. He backed up his proclamation of God's reign with many miracles and signs. He cured lepers, gave sight to the blind and hearing to the deaf. He fed the multitudes with a few loaves of bread and exorcised demons from the possessed.

Jesus' words and actions called for a decision from those who met him. He preached repentance, a complete turning from sin. He called people to have faith, to accept God's love, and to believe in him as God's special messenger.

His opponents were upset that he befriended such people as prostitutes and tax collectors. They also complained that he wanted to abolish the Law, because he criticized their detailed interpretations of it. They especially rejected his claims to speak for God. After all, in their eyes he was just an ordinary carpenter from Nazareth. They didn't like Jesus claiming divine authority:

> That made the Jews even more intent on killing him, because not only was he breaking the Sabbath, but he spoke of God as his own Father and so made himself God's equal (Jn 5:18).

Jesus did not flee from the plan to arrest him. Throughout his public ministry and at his last supper with the apostles, Jesus predicted his passion and death. He told his supporters that his death would be a supreme act of love for the remission of sins and the salvation of everyone.

One of his own apostles betrayed him, another denied knowing him, and most of the others abandoned him at the time of his arrest. The Jewish leaders tried him and accused him of blasphemy because he claimed to be God's Son. They turned him over to the Roman governor, Pontius Pilate, who tried, scourged, and crucified him as a seditionist, a so-called "King of the Jews."

At first, Jesus' humiliating and painful death on the cross made him appear to be a failure. The disciples were disillusioned; their faith was shattered. When the resurrection took place, however, a new era in human history began.

---

## Who Is Jesus for You?

Below are some statements that people make about Jesus. Check off those that you truly believe.

[ ] a nice guy
[ ] a deluded prophet
[ ] the Lord of the universe
[ ] a magician
[ ] a healer
[ ] Superman
[ ] Redeemer of humanity
[ ] the Savior of the world
[ ] a simple teacher of morality
[ ] Son of the Living God
[ ] a myth made up by the apostles
[ ] only a man
[ ] the promised Messiah
[ ] a fanatic Jew

### *discuss*

Using the list above or others that the class creates, discuss how the media (TV, movies, radio, music, advertising, etc.) depict Jesus.

### *journal*

Complete the following sentence and write a paragraph explaining your answer. Share this in class.

For me, Jesus is...

---

*Stage 2: Oral Tradition.* After Jesus' resurrection, he gave his followers the gift of the Holy Spirit. Through this Spirit, the apostles and disciples began to discover the true meaning of Jesus' life. Their lives became joyful celebrations of the risen Lord present in their midst.

The apostles remembered Jesus' command: "Go out to the whole world; proclaim the gospel to all creation" (Mk 16:16). They began to announce the marvelous things God had accomplished in Jesus. The early Christians remained pious Jews, believing that Jesus was the promised Messiah, the new covenant, the fulfillment of God's promises to the Chosen People. Because Jesus had commanded them to preach to all nations, Christians, under the leadership of Paul, began to preach throughout the Roman Empire. At first, their preaching was only to the Jews, but eventually, sometimes after being rejected by the Jews, the Christian missionaries preached to non-Jews or Gentiles.

The preaching took three forms in this period of oral tradition:

*1. Preaching to unbelievers.* The disciples would have kept in mind a basic outline of Jesus' works, his death, resurrection, and ascension. They would also have used many passages from the Hebrew scriptures to show how the prophecies made about the Messiah were fulfilled in Jesus. Finally, they may have assembled lists of various miracles and parables of Jesus to help them preach their message. Acts of the Apostles provides several sermons that Peter and Paul preached about Jesus.

This preaching is known as the *kerygma,* the essential message of salvation through the life, death, and resurrection of Jesus Christ.

---

## Kerygmatic Sermon

Please read *Acts 2* — Peter's proclamation on Pentecost Sunday. Complete the outline of the sermon given below:

1. The apostles are not drunk! Why?

______________________________________________

2. A review of Jesus' marvelous deeds.
3. The Jews and Romans put Jesus to death.
4. What does Peter say had been prophesied?

_______________________________________________

5. The Spirit has come in power.
6. What should his hearers do next?

_______________________________________________

---

*2. The* didache, *or teaching.* This teaching was further instruction for those who accepted Jesus. *Catechesis* repeats the message and explains it in more depth. Early converts needed further knowledge about how to live a more Christ-filled life. Sayings of Jesus, such as the Sermon on the Mount, were probably assembled to help in this instruction.

*3. The liturgy, or Christian worship.* The way people pray reflects their beliefs. The celebration of the eucharist helped shape many of the Jesus stories that the Christian community preserved. Certain key events, teachings, and prayers of Jesus were recalled in the early eucharistic celebrations. Some examples include Jesus' words at the Last Supper, the Lord's Prayer, and the story of Jesus' passion.

The Jesus material that was proclaimed, taught, and celebrated was shaped by different Christian communities. The early preachers' and teachers' primary interest was to interpret the *meaning* of the key events, deeds, and sayings of Jesus. They wanted to enliven the faith of the early Christians. As a result, they did not set out to report objective biographical sketches of Jesus. What they remembered, saved, and proclaimed was the heart of Jesus' message related to the Hebrew scriptures and adapted to the audiences who heard it.

*Stage 3: Written Letters and Gospels.* The final stage in the process was to write Jesus' gospel and various directions for Christian living. The earliest writings are the letters of St. Paul. Then came the four gospels and other writings such as the Acts and the book of Revelation.

Three things prompted the early Christians to commit their preaching to writing:

1. *The end of the world was not coming as quickly as the early Christians at first thought.* The first generation of Christians believed that Jesus would return "to judge the living and the dead" sometime in their lifetimes. As a result, they did not bother to write their testimony down. It was more urgent to preach the gospel and prepare for the Lord's return. They began to discover, however, that they were mistaken about the time of Christ's Second Coming. Eyewitnesses began to die or, even worse, be put to death. It became increasingly necessary to preserve in a more accurate and lasting manner the stories and testimony concerning Jesus.

2. *Distortions were arising.* The Christian scriptures themselves give evidence that often after the apostles preached in a certain community, others would begin to distort their message. In 2 Thessalonians, for example, Paul scolds some of his new converts. Apparently, they stopped working because they thought Jesus was going to return soon. Their idleness caused dissension in the community. So Paul advised them:

> Now we hear that there are some of you who are living lives without any discipline, doing no work themselves but interfering with other people's. In the Lord Jesus Christ, we urge and call on people of this kind to go on quietly working and earning the food that they eat.
>
> My brothers, never slacken in doing what is right. If anyone refuses to obey what I have written in this letter, take note of him and have nothing to do with him, so that he will be ashamed of himself, though you are not to treat him as an enemy, but to correct him as a brother (2 Thes 3:11–15).

3. *More instruction was needed.* A written record of the apostles' preaching could serve as a handy teaching device for Christians who needed more instruction. Writings could also serve as helpful guides in worship services. Finally, the church could circulate writings such as Paul's letters to the growing Christian communities. These writings provided a source for further instruction and, thus, helped new converts maintain proper belief.

*Inspired Writings.* Christians believe that God inspired both the Christian and the Hebrew scriptures. *Inspiration* means that the Holy Spirit authored the Bible through the individual talents and insights of the various human writers. The Second Vatican Council teaches:

> In composing the sacred books, God chose men and while employed by Him they made use of their powers and abilities, so that with Him acting in them and through them, they, as true authors, consigned to writing everything and only those things which He wanted (*Constitution on Divine Revelation*, No. 11).

We see this very vividly, for example, in the gospels. We have four versions of the one gospel, the good news of Jesus. Each *evangelist* — gospel writer — was a unique artist commissioned by the early Christian community to offer a unique and inspired portrait of Jesus. In addition, he was writing for a particular group of first-century Christians and so slanted his materials to speak to their unique needs. He creatively organized the written and oral sources available to him to underscore certain theological themes. Throughout this process of adapting, editing, and organizing, the Holy Spirit was at work to make sure that what the evangelist wrote was "the gospel truth."

*Canon of the New Testament.* The Greek word *kanon* literally means "measuring rod"; later it came to mean "rule" or "norm." The New Testament canon refers to the official list of twenty-seven inspired books. The church considers these books the rule or norm for its teaching. Today, Catholic, Orthodox, and Protestant churches all accept the same canon of New Testament books.

The history of the development of the canon is complex. For now, let us simply say that by the year 200, the gospels, Paul's epistles, Acts, and some other epistles were generally accepted as inspired. By the year 367, St. Athanasius fixed the canon at our present twenty-seven books. The Council of Trent (1545–1563) taught as a matter of church doctrine that this canon was the inspired word God left with the church.

The church included in the canon those writings that met three criteria:

1) they derive from the apostles;
2) they had wide circulation and acceptance throughout the various churches;
3) they reflected the traditional faith of the early Christian community.

---

## Books of the New Testament

(With Approximate Dates of Composition)

| *Gospels* | |
|---|---|
| Mark | 65–70 |
| Matthew | 70s–80s |
| Luke | 70s–80s |
| John | 90s |

| *Letters to All Christians* | |
|---|---|
| James | 62 (or 70s–80s) |
| 1 Peter | 64 (or 70s–80s) |
| Jude | 70s–90s |
| 1 John | 90s |
| 2 John | 90s |
| 3 John | 90s |
| 2 Peter | 100–150 |

| *Other Writings* | |
|---|---|
| Acts | 70s–80s |
| Hebrews | 60s–80s |
| Revelation | 90s |

| *Letters by Paul* | |
|---|---|
| 1 Thessalonians | 50 or 51 |
| Galatians | 54 |
| 1 Corinthians | 54 |
| 2 Corinthians | 55 |
| Philemon | 56–57 |
| Philippians | 57–58 |
| Romans | 57–58 |

| *Letters Attributed to Paul* | |
|---|---|
| Colossians | 61–63 or 70–80 |
| Ephesians | 61–63 or 90–100 |
| 2 Thessalonians | 90s |
| Titus | 95–100 |
| 1 Timothy | 95–100 |
| 2 Timothy | 95–100 |

*Note*: Scholars disagree among themselves over the dating of New Testament writings. The dates given here are suggested by *The New Jerome Biblical Commentary*.

### journal

Check your copy of the New Testament. Write the name of each book of the New Testament *with its abbreviation* into your journal.

---

# Background Helps for Reading the New Testament

*Languages and Texts of the New Testament.* If you lived in Israel in Jesus' day you might have heard four different spoken languages: Hebrew, Aramaic, Greek, and Latin. Hebrew was the ancient language of the Jewish people, the language in which most of the Hebrew scriptures were written. Educated Jews learned it to understand and pray the sacred scriptures, but it was no longer spoken by the ordinary people of the day. Rather, the ordinary Jew of Jesus' day spoke Aramaic, which became the common language of the Jewish people around the time of the Babylonian Captivity. Jesus spoke Aramaic, a richly poetic language. Some words of his native tongue appear in our Bible today: *Abba* (Mk 14:36), *Talitha kum* (Mk 5:41), and *Eloi, eloi, lama sabachthani* (Mk 15:34).

Alexander the Great's conquests of the Near East in the second half of the fourth century B.C. introduced Greek into the area. It quickly became the official language of business and government. Educated Romans admired and spoke Greek and for centuries it remained the official language of the Empire.

Because of the spread of Christianity beyond the borders of Israel, the early Christian writers decided to write in the language most people would understand: *koine* ("common") Greek. Koine Greek, spoken widely throughout the Roman Empire, is a fresh, warm, earthy language, though not as polished and refined as classical Greek.

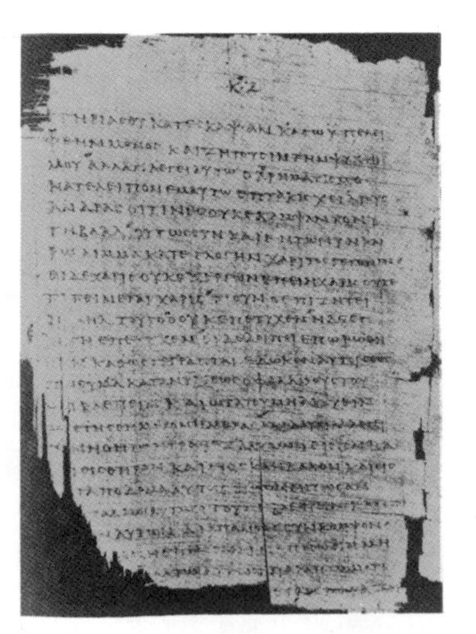

At first, scribes wrote on papyrus, a kind of paper made from a reed found in the delta of the Nile River and parts of Italy. Other writing was done on parchment made from the skins of animals. We can find papyri and parchments of the Christian scriptures in various libraries around the world. *Codex Vaticanus* is the oldest (c. A.D. 350) of all the important early collections of Christian writings. Two of the most famous papyri are the John Rylands Greek Papyrus and the Papyrus Bodmer.

*Translations.* St. Jerome, in the late fourth century, made a most significant translation of both the Old and New Testaments into Latin. Jerome's translation of the Bible, known as the *Vulgate* (meaning "common"), became the church's official translation.

Today, we read the Bible in our own language. There are many English translations, some under Catholic sponsorship, others under Protestant sponsorship.

Until this century, Catholics relied heavily on the Douay-Rheims Version (1582–1609) and its revision done by Bishop Challoner (1749–1763). The Douay Bible was a translation of the Latin Vulgate. In 1943, Pope Pius XII encouraged the translation of the Bible from the original languages. Two very popular and important English translations by Catholic scholars include:

1. *New American Bible* (1952–70; 1986). The church uses this translation for the readings at liturgies in the United States. It is solid, faithful to the original text, readable, and scholarly.

2. *Jerusalem Bible* (1966; 1985). The first edition of the Jerusalem Bible was an excellent translation of the French *Bible de Jérusalem*, which in turn was an important and scholarly translation from the original languages. The 1985 version translates the biblical texts directly from the original languages into English. It also includes the thorough and helpful introductions and notes from the French edition. *Living the Message of the New Testament* uses the Jerusalem Bible for the passages it quotes.

*Tools for Studying the Bible.* A *concordance* is an excellent tool for your Bible study. It lists all the occurrences of a word in the Bible. Suppose you cannot remember where Jesus said, "You are the light of the world." You could look up the word *light* in your concordance and find all the places it occurs in the Bible. Some Bibles include a short concordance of key words in an appendix. You can also find relatively inexpensive computer programs that will do searches for every word in the Bible. One caution: You should use a concordance that matches the translation of the Bible you are reading.

A good *Bible atlas* will provide some maps of the New Testament world. Also, be sure to check the maps provided with many Bibles. For example, the *Jerusalem Bible* contains eight excellent maps.

Most libraries contain several solid *Bible dictionaries*. These reference works treat many themes, names, places, and other topics found in the Bible.

A helpful work entitled *Gospel Parallels* lines up parallel passages in the gospels side by side so you can compare one evangelist's version with another. This is a helpful research tool especially when you are studying the synoptic gospels — Matthew, Mark, and Luke.

There are many excellent *commentaries* on all the books of the Bible. While some of these commentaries are quite scholarly, others can be understood by even the beginning Bible student. One excellent series is the *Collegeville Bible Commentary*, available in a multi-volume set or as one volume. Another outstanding one-volume commentary on the entire Bible, edited by several renowned Catholic scholars, is *The New Jerome Biblical Commentary*.

## ▪ focus questions ▪

1. How many books does the New Testament contain? What are three major groupings represented in this collection?
2. What is the meaning of the word *testament*? Explain the relationship between the Hebrew scriptures and the New Testament.
3. Briefly discuss some highlights of Yahweh's covenant relationship with the Jewish people.
4. Which Jewish king symbolized the hope for a promised Messiah?
5. In what way is Jesus God's new covenant with all people?
6. What were the three stages (with their dates) in the formation of the Christian scriptures?
7. When was Jesus born? When did he die?
8. Summarize in one sentence the essential message of Jesus during his public life. How did he back up his preaching?
9. Why did Jesus allow himself to be crucified?
10. Why did the apostles and disciples preach beyond the borders of Israel?
11. Briefly discuss three forms that apostolic preaching took during the period of oral tradition.
12. Discuss why first-generation Christians eventually wrote down the gospels.
13. What do we mean when we say the scriptures are *inspired*?

14. What were the criteria for accepting a particular writing into the New Testament canon?
15. What language did Jesus speak? In what language were all the books of the New Testament written? Why?
16. List two contemporary English translations of the Bible.
17. What biblical reference work could you consult if you wanted to...
    a. understand the meaning of Mt 6:33–34?
    b. locate Nazareth in relationship to Capernaum?
    c. find the meaning of the word *Amen*?
    d. compare Luke's version of the Lord's Prayer with Matthew's?
    e. find out where in the gospels Jesus said, "Come after me and I will make you fishers of people?"
18. Briefly identify the following terms:

| | | |
|---|---|---|
| canon (of the Bible) | Exodus | kerygma |
| catechesis | hesed | koine |
| didache | inspiration | Vulgate |

## ▪ exercises ▪

1. Consult a concordance and find one reference in each of the gospels in which Jesus uses the expression "kingdom of God" (or "reign of God").
2. Consult a biblical dictionary and prepare a report on one of the following topics:
    a. the profession of a scribe in Jesus' day
    b. who the twelve apostles were and what their mission was
    c. a brief report on the canon of the New Testament
3. Consult a Bible atlas and locate these cities:

- Ephesus
- Tarsus
- Thessalonica
- Magdala
- Bethlehem

### ▪ vocabulary ▪

**Copy the meaning of these words into the vocabulary section of your journal:**

**apocalypse**
**ascribe**
**dissolute**
**seditionist**

4. Locate a commentary on Matthew's gospel. What does the commentator say is the meaning of Mt 6:33–34?
5. Read a commentary on Acts 2:14–41.

## Prayer Reflection

St. Paul included many prayers and blessings in his letters. They can teach us a lot about how to approach God. In the very first Christian writing — 1 Thessalonians — Paul writes:

> Always be joyful; pray constantly; and for all things give thanks; this is the will of God for you in Christ Jesus.
>
> May the God of peace make you perfect and holy; and may your spirit, life and body be kept blameless for the coming of our Lord Jesus Christ. He who has called you is trustworthy and will carry it out.
>
> The grace of our Lord Jesus Christ be with you.
>
> — 1 Thes 5:16–18; 23–24; 28

### reflection

How is your prayer life? Do you pray constantly as St. Paul instructs?

### resolution

Construct a list of things and people for which you are or should be thankful. Approach our Lord with joy in your heart and thank him for his many blessings.

*chapter* 2

# The World of Jesus' Day

In the fifteenth year of Tiberius Caesar's reign, when Pontius Pilate was governor of Judea, Herod tetrarch of Galilee, his brother Philip tetrarch of the territories of Ituraea and Trachonitis, Lysanias tetrarch of Abilene, and while the high-priesthood was held by Annas and Caiaphas, the word of God came to John the son of Zechariah, in the desert.

— Luke 3:1–2

**In This Chapter**

**We will look at:**

- **the Holy Land**
- **the political scene**
- **first century Jewish beliefs**
- **religious groups in Jesus' day**

*"He was a young man born in an obscure village, the child of a peasant woman. He grew up in still another village. He worked in a carpenter shop until he was thirty, and then for three years he was an itinerant preacher. He never wrote a book, held an office, or owned a home. He never lived in a big city. He never travelled more than two hundred miles from where he was born. He never did any of the things that usually accompany greatness. He had no credentials but himself.*

*"While he was still a young man, the tide of public opinion turned against him. His friends ran away. He was turned over to his enemies. He went through a mockery of a trial. He was nailed to a cross between two thieves. While he was dying, his executioners gambled for the only piece of property he had on earth, his coat. When he was dead, he was laid in a borrowed tomb.*

*"Nearly twenty centuries have come and gone, and today he is the central figure of the human race. All the armies that ever marched, all the navies that ever sailed, all the governments that ever sat, and all the kings that ever reigned, put together, have not affected human life on this earth as has that one solitary life" (Anonymous).*

Jesus lived among us as a man of his people. Around the age of thirty, he began his public ministry of teaching and healing, proclaiming God's goodness and salvation in word and deed. The scripture quote that opens this chapter reminds us that Jesus' ministry took place at a particular time and in a particular place. It began with his baptism by John and lasted about three years. Luke mentions the Roman occupation of Palestine in the first century. He also identifies the Jewish high priest at the beginning of Jesus' ministry. Facts such as these underscore Jesus' reality as a *historical* person. The world he lived in, although different from our own, was very real. We will examine some important features of this world. The more we appreciate the political, social, cultural, and religious environment that gave birth to the Christian scriptures, the more we will gain from reading them.

## Mystery of Love

In the New Testament we read the story of God's love for us in the life of Jesus of Nazareth. The reality of this love for each of us is beyond the grasp of our intellects. The life of Jesus seems to contradict everything our society tells us will lead to success and happiness. And yet Christians believe that the mystery of God's love, and the person of Jesus, are the most significant realities in their lives.

Reflect on the many truths revealed in the New Testament. Rate your current level of belief concerning each of the following statements. Use the following scale:

1 — has great meaning for me
2 — I'm lukewarm on this
3 — my faith needs much strengthening

1. God loves me unconditionally as a unique individual of great worth.

   1 2 3

2. God loves everyone with a tremendous love. Everyone is my brother or sister in the Lord.

   1 2 3

3. God has destined me for abundant life with him in eternity.

   1 2 3

4. God wants me to accept his love. To do so I should repent of anything that keeps me away from him.

   1 2 3

5. Jesus is God the Father's gift to me. He is *the* sign of God's love made flesh. He is my friend and Savior.

   1 2 3

6. The Holy Spirit opens me up to God's love and truth. The Spirit has blessed me with gifts to live a Christ-like life.

   1 2 3

7. Jesus reveals that the way to life is for me to die to myself, that is, sacrifice, love, and serve.

   1 2 3

8. My life is filled with hope because I believe Jesus' message that good will triumph over evil, that life will conquer death.

   1 2 3

**■ discuss ■**

What characteristics does our society think are necessary for success? Which of these characteristics did Jesus possess? Which ones did he clearly *not* possess?

**■ journal ■**

**Think about the characteristics of a socially successful person that you already possess. Which ones are you working to attain? Write a few sentences about your goals, about your idea of a successful life. Then reread the story that opens the chapter. Do you really want to be like Jesus?**

## The Holy Land

Jews at the time of Jesus spoke of their beloved country as the Promised Land, the Land of Israel, the Land of Judah, or simply the Land. The Greeks, on the other hand, referred to it as Palestine after the Philistines, the seafaring pirates who lived in the northern coastal areas. (The Jews hated this name for their land.) Roughly the shape of a rectangle, this land stretches 145 miles north to south and from 25 miles wide in the north to its greatest width of 87 miles near the Dead Sea in the south. This area has always held a strategic place in world history. It served as the crossroads for Egyptian, Syrian, and Persian expansions. Later, it became an attractive target for the political conquests of Greece and Rome.

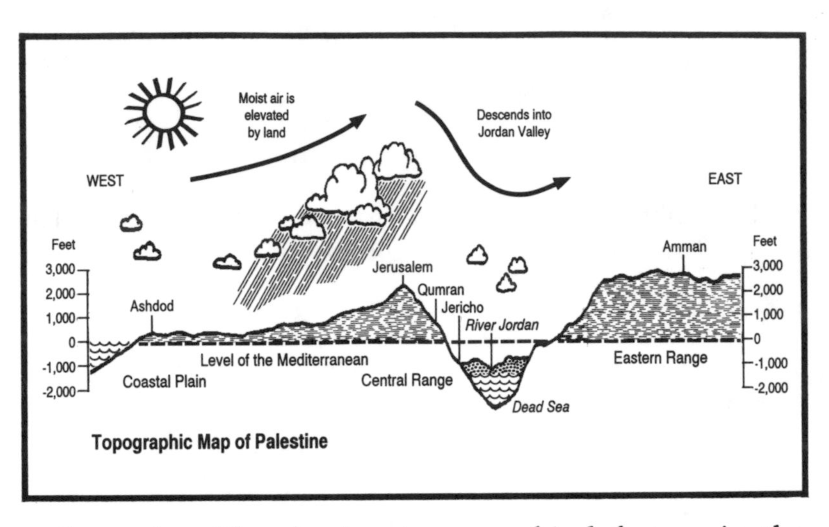

**Topographic Map of Palestine**

*Geography.* The dominant geographical feature in the Holy Land is a mountain range running north and south. About fifty miles inland, it parallels the Mediterranean seacoast. On the crest of this chain the Jews built some of their principal cities, including Jerusalem.

East of the mountains the land falls sharply into the valley of the Jordan River. This river, rising in the northern mountains, widens into the freshwater Sea of Galilee and then narrows into a fertile valley on its way to the saltiest of all bodies of water — the Dead Sea. This body of water is the lowest point on the face of the earth, 1200 feet below sea level. The Dead Sea has a salt content of 25 percent, six times that of the saltiest ocean. It is impossible to sink in it.

*Regions and Cities.* The three key regions of interest at the time of Jesus' ministry were Galilee, Samaria, and Judea.

*Galilee* in the northwest was a land of fertile, rolling hills watered by the Jordan River and the Sea of Galilee. Farmers and shepherds prospered in this region. The sea also provided a livelihood for many fishermen. The population was mainly Jewish, but many non-Jews could also be found in the area.

Jesus was a Galilean, as were most of his apostles. He grew up in Nazareth, a small town of about 1200 people. It lay two miles off the main road through southern Galilee. Other cities in Galilee that were important in Jesus' ministry include Capernaum, Cana, and Bethsaida.

The region of *Samaria* lies to the south of Galilee. The Samaritans numbered among their ancestors the foreigners who came into Palestine at the time of Assyria's conquest

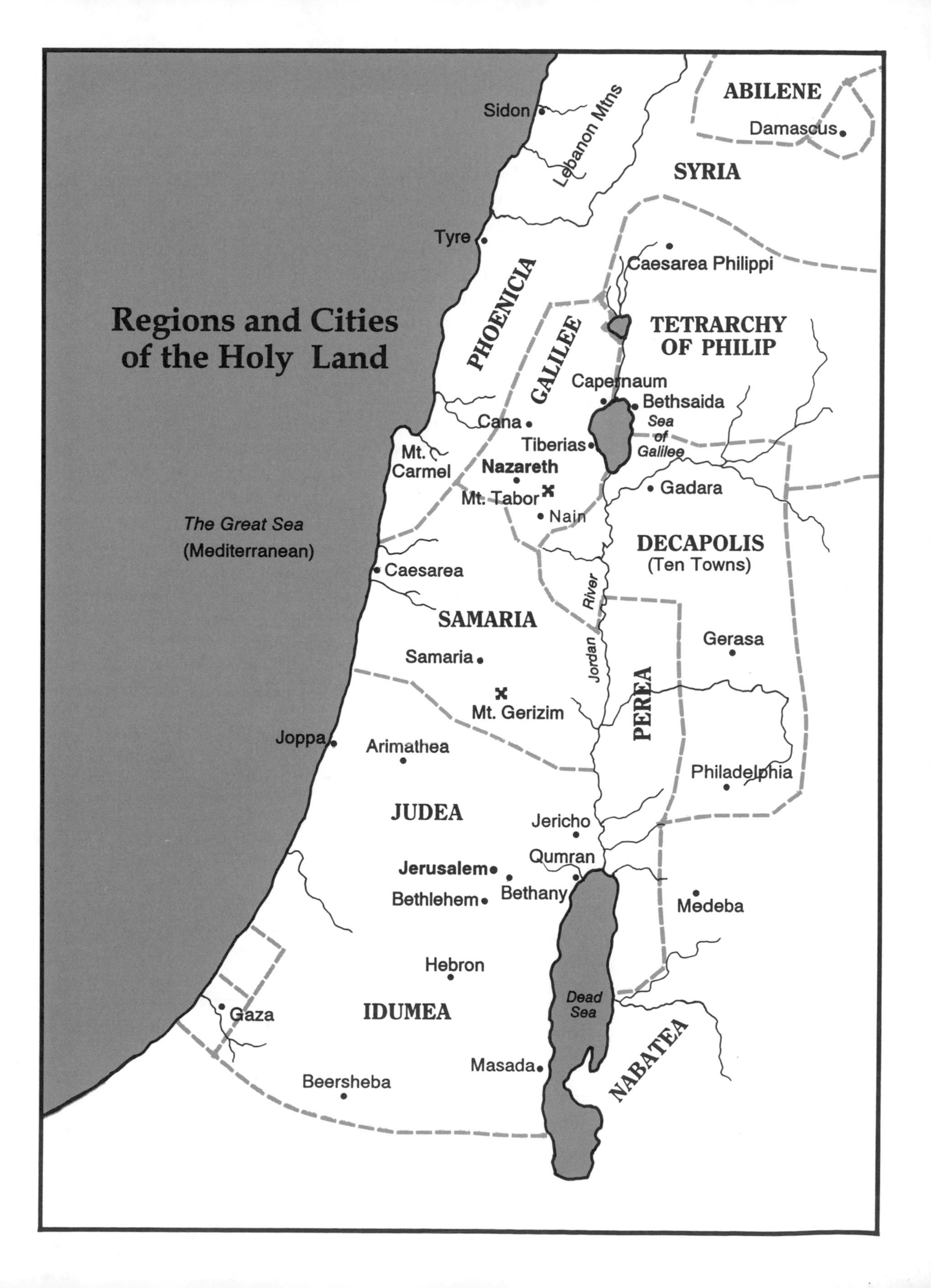

Regions and Cities of the Holy Land
ABILENE
Damascus
Sidon
Lebanon Mtns
SYRIA
Tyre
Caesarea Philippi
PHOENICIA
GALILEE
TETRARCHY OF PHILIP
Capernaum
Bethsaida
Sea of Galilee
Cana
Tiberias
Mt. Carmel
Nazareth
Mt. Tabor
Gadara
Nain
The Great Sea
(Mediterranean)
DECAPOLIS
(Ten Towns)
Caesarea
River
SAMARIA
Gerasa
Samaria
Jordan
PEREA
Mt. Gerizim
Joppa
Arimathea
Philadelphia
JUDEA
Jericho
Qumran
Jerusalem
Bethany
Bethlehem
Medeba
Hebron
Dead Sea
Gaza
IDUMEA
NABATEA
Masada
Beersheba

of the northern kingdom. The Samaritans accepted the Law of Moses and the belief in one God, though they rejected the writings of the prophets and the wisdom writings. They also rejected the Temple in Jerusalem as the center of Jewish worship. They constructed their own shrine on Mount Gerizim. For these reasons the Jews looked on Samaritan worship as false.

Relations between the Samaritans and Jews were strained; Jews considered them heretical and hated them even more than pagans. Jesus' loving attitude toward Samaritans upset many of his contemporaries.

*Judea* in the south was a dry, barren, craggy land. Its main inhabitants were the Jews who returned after the captivity in Babylon. The leaders of the Jewish people had all settled here. In the center of Judea, high on two hills 2255 to 2400 feet above sea level, was *Jerusalem*, the political, economic, and religious center. Most of the Judean population lived in this city and also in Jericho. Southern Judea and the Dead Sea area were desert. Jesus retreated here after his baptism (Mt 4:1). Other cities in Judea that are significant to Jesus' story are Bethlehem and Bethany.

## Places in Jesus' Ministry

Check the following passages and answer the questions asked.

a. Where did Jesus eat a meal with two disciples after the resurrection? (Lk 24:13)

________________________________________

b. Where were Jesus and the apostles going when Peter proclaimed Jesus as Messiah? (Mk 8:27–33)

________________________________________

c. To which city was the traveler in the parable of the good Samaritan going? (Lk 10:30)

________________________________________

d. Where did Jesus meet a woman and reveal that he was the living water? (Jn 4:5)

________________________________________

e. Where did Jesus heal Peter's mother-in-law? (Mk 1:21, 29–31)

______________________________________________

---

*Religious Practices.* For the Jews there was only one Temple and it was in Jerusalem. The Temple was a holy place where they offered sacrifice to God and where they thought God dwelled in a special way. Only the priestly caste had a role in Temple worship, sacrificing animals to Yahweh on a daily basis. And only the high priest could enter the Holy of Holies once a year, on *Yom Kippur*, the Day of Atonement.

The Temple standing during New Testament times was the third one constructed in Jerusalem. The first, Solomon's, stood for four hundred years before it was destroyed by the Babylonians in 587 B.C. The second temple, that of Zerubbabel, was more modest. Construction of Herod the Great's magnificent Temple began in 19 B.C. and was finished ten years later, although the work of decorating the Temple was still going on in Jesus' day. It was completely finished in A.D. 64, only six years before the Romans levelled it during the Jewish Revolt (66–70).

It was a marvelous structure, 2350 feet at its perimeter, with eight main gates. Around the altar was a courtyard reserved for priests. Next was the courtyard of Israel (for men) and then the courtyard for women. Beyond that was the courtyard of the Gentiles.

The Law required people to pay a Temple tax and obligated Jewish men to make a pilgrimage to Jerusalem on the major religious feasts, although not all Jews could make it to the holy city for all the feasts.

The most important feast was Passover, which celebrated Jewish liberation from Egypt, the Exodus. Perhaps 200,000 pilgrims came to Jerusalem for this feast. Each year the Jewish people commemorated this event with a special meal called a seder.

Jesus learned his Jewish religion in Nazareth's *synagogue*, a prayer meeting house that was found in every Jewish community of ten or more men. Many larger towns had more than one synagogue and Jerusalem may have had hundreds. The synagogue — which also meant the assembly of gathered people — served three purposes: 1) it was a house of prayer and worship; 2) it served as a place of discussion for legal settlements; 3) it was the local school. Jesus typically proclaimed his message in synagogues. So did Paul and other early Christian missionaries who tried to point out how Jesus fulfilled the prophecies of the Hebrew scriptures.

■ research ■

Using a biblical dictionary, research one of the following topics and prepare a short report:

a. one of the major Jewish feasts: Passover, Tabernacles, Pentecost, Yom Kippur, or Hannukah
b. history of the Jerusalem Temple
c. an important city in the Holy Land

## The Political Scene

When Jesus was born, Palestine was part of the Roman Empire, which extended from Great Britain in northern Europe to Egypt in the southeastern part of the Mediterranean basin. The so-called *Pax Romana* — the Peace of Rome — was in effect, which meant that the entire region was united under a single rule and no wars were taking place anywhere in the Empire. This brought several benefits: a common language, an intricate system of roads, a good system of justice, and a strong military force.

Most Jews, however, hated Roman rule. For almost six centuries, Israel had been under foreign rulers: Babylonians, Persians, Greeks, Seleucids. Finally, in 63 B.C., the Romans under General Pompey came to Palestine. At first, Rome permitted the Jews a limited self-rule under Herod the Great. Herod was a cunning, crafty, and, in many ways, cruel ruler. Matthew's story about the slaughter of the innocents at the time of Jesus' birth, though not documented in other sources, certainly fits Herod's character. The Jewish historian Josephus tells us that Herod slaughtered several of his sons, a wife (he had ten!), and several other relatives for fear that they might usurp his throne.

Herod courted the favor of the emperor by constructing many buildings throughout his domain and then dedicating them to the emperor. He even erected pagan temples and supported emperor worship. This was an abomination to the

Jews. Though "King of the Jews," he was no Jewish king. Herod redeemed himself somewhat in the eyes of his Jewish subjects by undertaking the construction of the magnificent Temple in Jerusalem.

Herod died in 4 B.C. Three of his sons divided the kingdom among them. Archelaus (4 B.C.-A.D. 6) gained most of Samaria, Idumea, and Judea. Herod Antipas (4 B.C.-A.D. 39) ruled Perea and Galilee, Jesus' home province. Herod Antipas reigned throughout most of Jesus' life. He was the one who executed John the Baptist because John criticized Antipas' adulterous relationship with his half-brother Philip's wife, Herodias. He also played an instrumental part in the arrest and trial of Jesus. Finally, Philip (4 B.C.-A.D. 34) controlled the lands to the north and east of the sea of Galilee.

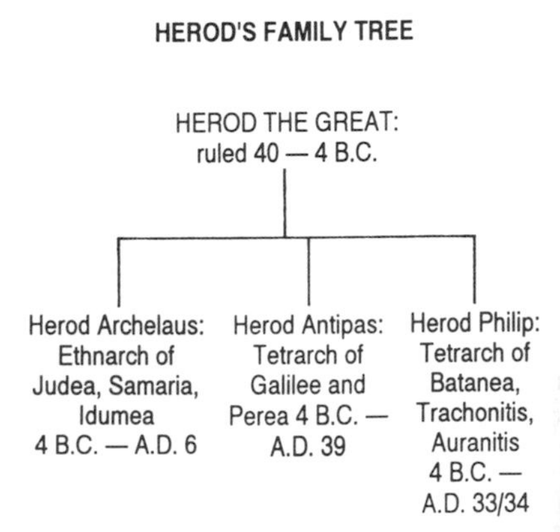


Archelaus was a bloodthirsty ruler, killing three thousand of his subjects within months of gaining power. He was extremely unpopular with his subjects, who badgered Rome to remove him. After nine years of complaints, Rome deposed Archelaus and in his place appointed a prefect directly answerable to the Roman governor in Syria. The New Testament mentions three Roman prefects: Pontius Pilate (26–36), Felix (52–60), and Festus (60–62).

The Roman prefect's main tasks were collecting taxes, confirming death sentences imposed by the Jewish court, keeping the peace, and reporting to Rome about the general state of affairs. He had the power to appoint and depose the Jewish high priest, who controlled Temple worship and so had a great influence on the people. He also commanded auxiliary forces in Judea made up of non-Jewish residents of Palestine and Syria. Jews greatly resented these troops. They especially hated Jewish tax collectors who collaborated with the Romans in exacting taxes.

Pilate, the Roman prefect who passed sentence on Jesus, was a high-handed, stern ruler who did nothing to endear himself to the Jews. Ruling from the seacoast town of Caesarea, he had military standards bearing the emperor's image erected in Jerusalem, an act that outraged pious Jews because Yahweh forbade graven images. Pilate also robbed the Temple treasury to build an aqueduct. When the Jews protested, he disguised some of his men and had them infiltrate a protesting crowd. At a predesignated signal, they drew their swords and slaughtered many of the defenseless Jews.

According to one of his political enemies, Pilate was guilty of "graft, insults, robberies, assaults, wanton abuse, constant executions without trial, unending grievous cruelty." He was eventually recalled to Rome and probably exiled to Gaul.

Even though Rome allowed the Jews considerable freedom in practicing their religion, its rule was harsh and all Jews longed for the day when a Messiah would come to deliver them.

▪ *journal* ▪

Acts reveals many interesting insights into Roman life. Please read Acts 16:16–40 and answer these questions in your journal.

1. What was the occupation of the slave girl in this passage?
2. Why were Paul and Silas arrested?
3. What happened while they were in prison? Why did the jailer wish to kill himself? Describe his conversion.
4. How was Roman justice violated in this case?

Consult a biblical atlas and locate Philippi on a map.

## First Century Jewish Beliefs

The New Testament has deep roots in the religious beliefs, practices, affiliations, and expectations of the Jewish people. Jesus himself was a pious Jew. Many of the first-century Christians were also Jewish, although their acceptance of Jesus as the Messiah set them apart from fellow Jews. Their first missionary task was to proclaim the good news that Yahweh had fulfilled his promises to the Jewish people in Jesus of Nazareth.

To better understand the New Testament writings, we need to look at some of the important beliefs of the early Jewish-Christians who produced most of the New Testament writings. We will also briefly introduce some of the various Jewish religious groups prominent in the New Testament world.

*The Messiah.* The New Testament period was high in "messianic expectations." Most Jews strongly believed that Yahweh would send a Messiah very soon. The Hebrew word *masiah* (messiah) is translated into Greek as *christos* (Christ) which literally means "anointed one." At first, the title *messiah* applied to God's chosen or anointed leader, the king. From the time of King David's reign (c. 1000 B.C.), the Jews believed that their covenant relationship with God meant that Yahweh would give them a king who would represent the love and care he had for his people. Unfortunately, most of David's successors were weak and corrupt, leading to the destruction of both the northern and southern kingdoms and the Babylonian exile.

Following the exile in Babylon, the Jews increasingly believed that the Messiah would usher in God's reign. Various groups in Jesus' day had different expectations of who or what the Messiah would be, but all of them expected a political leader like David who would lead Israel to military victory and re-establish the prominence of Israel. Many contemporaries of Jesus fully expected this to happen in a dramatic revelation of the Messiah's identity and a wondrous establishment of God's reign. Furthermore, God would restore Israel to its rightful place among the nations.

One reason so many of Jesus' contemporaries did not recognize or accept Jesus as the Messiah was that so much of what he did and said contradicted popular expectations. He was a carpenter from Nazareth, not a royal-looking figure. His message was not one of violence and war, but of peace and love. He taught love of enemies and associated with sinners. Jesus interpreted his role as Messiah as suffering for others. As Savior, he was the Suffering Servant, which even went against the thinking of his apostles until the Spirit enlightened them at Pentecost.

*The Reign of God.* The reign of God refers to the acceptance of God's will by everyone. It is a central theme in Jesus' teaching and in the faith of the Jewish people. When people know and accept Yahweh as he has revealed himself through the Jews and later most perfectly through Jesus Christ, then heaven and earth will meet. Justice will reign, material needs will be fulfilled, and God's peace (*shalom*) will embrace the whole world.

Christians believe Jesus both announces the coming of God's reign and also ushers it in. His life, healing ministry, teaching, and sacrifice on the cross have established God's reign once and for all. As his followers, Christians have Jesus' own mandate to help the reign of God grow and take hold in the hearts of people. We do this by worshipping God in truth, heralding the good news, living lovingly with others in community, and serving the needs of everyone, especially those who are hurting. The New Testament proclaims this message of God's reign again and again.

*The Torah.* Believing in and keeping the *Torah* or Law was the heart of Jewish life. The Pentateuch, the first five books of the Hebrew scriptures, contains the Torah. To the Jews, the Law is not a list of arbitrary rules, but God's self-revelation. It's what he expects as a response to his covenant love. He had created the Jews as a special people, promising to bless, guide, and protect them forever. In return they were to recognize Yahweh as the one true God and keep the Law.

Living the Law influenced every aspect of Jewish history, culture, morality, and worship. To be outside the Law was to draw judgment on oneself and the nation. Sects such as the Pharisees and the Essenes believed that God allowed foreign powers to dominate the Jews because so many people did not live the Law. They tried to live the law perfectly — and taught others to do the same — in the belief that Yahweh would have to respond by sending a Messiah to rescue them.

Jesus had profound respect for the Law and instructed his followers to keep it: "Do not imagine that I have come to abolish the Law or the Prophets. I have come not to abolish but to complete them" (Mt 5:17). The Torah is still at the heart of Jewish religious practice today.

*Judgment and Resurrection.* Since the second century B.C., most Jews believed that Yahweh would judge the dead by rewarding the good and punishing the evil. The prophet Daniel introduced the idea of the resurrection of good people who shall live forever: "Of those who are sleeping in the Land of Dust, many will awaken, some to everlasting life, some to shame and everlasting disgrace" (Dn 12:2).

Jesus, of course, accepted this view of human destiny, and Christians hold it as a core doctrine of faith. We believe that our resurrection will take place because we are one with the Lord who has conquered sin and death.

*Parousia.* The Jews linked together the coming of the Messiah with the reign of God. Because the early Christians accepted Jesus as the Christ, they believed that he would return in glory to establish the fullness of God's reign. This would take place at the *Parousia,* the Second Coming of Christ, an event the early Christians thought would happen in their lifetimes.

New Testament letters such as First and Second Thessalonians show that many Christians thought Jesus would return soon. Paul even held this belief for a time. The gospels give conflicting evidence about the Second Coming. In one passage, Jesus apparently states that it would happen in the lifetimes of the apostles (Mt 24:34); in another passage, Jesus says: "But as for that day and hour, nobody knows it, neither the angels of heaven, nor the Son, no one but the Father alone" (Mt 24:36). Even today we await the Parousia. The early Christians have joined the Lord in heaven while the church continues to spread his gospel to the ends of the earth.

*Spirit World.* It may not be fashionable today to believe in angels and devils, but people in New Testament times assumed their existence. From the earliest days, Jews believed in heavenly messengers (*angel* means "messenger"). In the time between the writing of the Old and New Testaments belief in angels grew. The New Testament frequently mentions both angels and devils. Jews believed that various demons warred against God by being the sources of sickness, temptation, and sin. Jesus cast out many demons and saw his own suffering as a war against the evil one — Satan (Jn 12:31). Although Jews and Christians accepted the existence of demons, they believed that they were subject to God.

# Religious Groups in Jesus' Day

Josephus, an important Jewish historian, tells us about some of the important religious groups that appear in the New Testament. In his history of the Jewish people, written in the latter part of the first century, Josephus mentions four sects or "philosophies": the Sadducees, the Pharisees, the Essenes, and the Zealots.

*Sadducees.* This religious sect got its name from Zadok, the priest whom Solomon appointed to take charge of the ark of the covenant (1 Kgs 2:35). They were priests and aristocrats who supervised Temple practices and worship. As a result, they centered their activities in Jerusalem. They collaborated with the Romans to stay in power.

Theologically conservative, the Sadducees accepted the Law (the Pentateuch) as inspired, but not the Prophets or other sacred writings such as the wisdom literature. They did not believe in the resurrection of the dead or in angels.

Many Sadducees, along with a few Pharisees, made up the seventy-one-member *Sanhedrin*, the major law-making body and supreme court of Judaism.

The Sadducees disappeared from the Jewish scene when the Temple was destroyed in 70. Without a Temple in which to center their power and influence, they lost both political and spiritual authority.

*Pharisees.* Although numbering perhaps only six thousand during Jesus' ministry, this Jewish sect had great influence. Jesus was probably closest to them in beliefs and spiritual practices. For example, both believed in the resurrection and divine judgment of the living and the dead. They also thought prayer, almsgiving, and fasting were essential spiritual practices.

The term *Pharisee* means "separated one." Pharisees came into existence during the Hasmonean dynasty (135–63 B.C.) when they separated themselves from the ordinary religious practices of that day. They believed in strict observance of the Law, which kept them from sin and Gentile influence. This group of laymen, many from the middle class, actively pursued holiness. They criticized Jesus for associating with people who didn't observe the Jewish Law. For example, tax collectors were considered to be notorious sinners. Most Jews hated any fellow Jew who would stoop so low as to work for the Romans. Moreover, the tax collectors often tried to line their own pockets at the expense of their fellow Jews. Jesus, however, not only associated with these despised people but even called one of them — Matthew (Levi) — to be an apostle.

There was much to admire in the Pharisees. Their religious devotions were positive practices that inspired many of their fellow Jews. Some Pharisees, though, were perhaps too eager to apply the Torah to daily life. They developed an elaborate system of oral interpretation, which they held to be almost as sacred as the Law itself. These oral traditions, however, sometimes missed the spirit of the Law. Jesus held the Law sacred, but he freed his followers from blind observance of laws that put human customs above the needs of people. He influenced people to do good without recourse to an elaborate system of minute observance of religious customs. Some Pharisees criticized Jesus for this.

Many Pharisees were *scribes,* experts in the Jewish Law. The New Testament portrays scribes as enemies of Jesus because he taught on his own unique authority. Scribes, on the other hand, cited the Law and scholarly interpretations of it as a sure way to holiness.

Jesus criticized some Pharisees because they thought they could earn heaven by keeping all their religious customs. Jesus taught that God's love and the reign of God are pure gift, bestowed on saint and sinner alike. Conflict between these two approaches to God's goodness was inevitable.

Although the Pharisees have a bad reputation in the New Testament, many of them were very good Jews. Some of them, most notably Paul, became staunch followers of Jesus.

The Pharisees saved the Jewish religion after the destruction of the Temple. Under the rabbi Jonathan ben Zakkai, some Pharisees regrouped at Jamnia (present-day Jabneh near Tel Aviv) and reformed Judaism. First, they formed a canon of sacred books, accepting only those written in Hebrew. They also established a liturgical calendar and unified synagogue worship.

The gathering at Jamnia also drove Christians out of Judaism. Tension between Jews and Jewish-Christians had been growing for decades. However, when Christians refused to fight the Romans in the First Revolt, the surviving Jews felt it was time to break with the Christian sect. They did this by introducing a petition in the synagogue prayer known as the Eighteen Benedictions. This prayer in effect cursed "heretics, apostates, and the proud," which included Christians.

Matthew's gospel reflects some of the animosity Jewish-Christians felt toward this move by the Pharisees, which helps explain why Pharisees have such a bad name in the gospels.

## Jesus and the Pharisees and Sadducees

The gospels often depict Jesus debating the Pharisees and Sadducees, who often tried to trap him. They tested and criticized Jesus. Read these two important passages where Jesus debated these groups. Answer the questions in your journal.

*Debate with the Pharisees: Mk 7:1–23*

1. What did the disciples fail to do? (vv. 1–2)
2. Why did the Pharisees think this was a problem? (vv. 3–6)
3. What commandment does Jesus say they try to avoid? (vv. 9–10)
4. How do the Pharisees excuse their obligation to keep this commandment? (vv. 11–18)
5. From where does evil come? (vv. 14–20)
6. List several actions that come from evil intentions. (v. 21)

*Debate with the Sadducees: Mk 12:18–27*

1. What case do the Sadducees put before Jesus? (vv. 19–23)
2. Who established the law quoted by the Sadducees? (v. 19)
3. Was the question to Jesus sincere? Why or why not? (v. 18)

Jesus responds to the Sadducees by giving them a two-part answer. First, he answers their question on its own merits.

4. What does Jesus say about marriage at the resurrection? (v. 25)

Second, Jesus shows that he believes in the resurrection by quoting a higher authority than the Sadducees.

5. Whom does Jesus quote in support of his belief? (v. 26) Whom had the Sadducees quoted? (v. 19)

**■ discuss ■**

**How does Jesus beat the Sadducees at their own game?**

*Essenes.* According to Josephus, this group, founded by a man called the Teacher of Righteousness, believed that the Jerusalem priesthood and Temple worship were impure and that most Jews failed to live the Law. As a result most of them withdrew to a desert community — at Qumran near the Dead Sea. They lived a celibate life, shared goods in common, and lived a life of ritual purity, cleansing themselves often throughout the day. We can see their ritual baths in the archaeological remains of the Qumran monastery.

Some scholars feel that John the Baptist may have been influenced by the Essenes. They believed God's reign would be revealed through a dramatic, even catastrophic event, most likely a great battle between the forces of good and the forces of evil. The Essenes carefully read and produced commentaries on the Hebrew scriptures hoping to find signs of the coming event. They lived strict lives, believing that they would be on Yahweh's side when the great day came. Like the Sadducees, the Essenes disappeared after the destruction of the Temple.

*Zealots.* The Zealots despised Roman rule and believed in violence to overthrow their enemies. The Zealots began as a group in Galilee to protest foreign taxation and occupation. They were active as Jesus grew up and during his public ministry. One of his apostles, Simon, was a Zealot. The Zealots eventually fomented the revolt against the Romans.

## ▪ focus questions ▪

1. Where did the Holy Land get the name *Palestine*?
2. Describe the geography of the Holy Land.
3. Discuss the principal regions of the Holy Land that figured prominently in Jesus' ministry.
4. What role did the synagogue play in Jewish life? What role did it play in the ministries of St. Paul and Jesus?
5. What was the attitude of Jews toward Samaritans? Who were the Samaritans?
6. Why was the Temple central to Jewish life? Describe its construction.
7. Explain the Jewish feast of Passover.
8. What were some advantages of the *Pax Romana*?

9. From a Jewish point of view, what was Herod the Great's finest accomplishment?
10. What was the role of the Roman prefects/procurators in Palestine? Characterize Pontius Pilate.
11. Explain the messianic expectations of the first century. Did Jesus fit the popular ideas Jews had of the Messiah? Explain.
12. What does the New Testament mean by the term "reign of God"? How is this theme central to the preaching of the early Christians?
13. What role did the Torah play in Jewish life? What was Jesus' attitude to it?
14. What did first-century Jews and Christians believe about angels and devils?
15. Distinguish between the following Jewish sects: Pharisee, Sadducee, Essene, Zealot. Discuss a key belief of each.
16. Briefly identify the following terms, places, and people:

    Parousia
    scribe
    Sanhedrin
    Josephus
    Jonathan ben Zakkai
    Qumran
    Herod the Great
    Archelaus
    Herod Antipas

## ■ exercises ■

1. Consult a biblical dictionary or other background books on the New Testament and prepare a report on one of the following topics:
    a. Sadducees, Pharisees, Zealots, or Essenes
    b. the Dead Sea Scrolls
    c. the First Revolt
2. Draw a floor plan of Herod's Temple.
3. Interview a rabbi (or do other research) to find out how a synagogue service is conducted today.

## ■ vocabulary ■

**Write the definitions of these words in your journal:**

**atonement**
**endear**
**foment**

## ■ journal ■

Read the following passages and summarize your findings.

a. Read Lk 7:36–50 and Acts 5:34–39. Contrast the words, thoughts, and behavior of these two Pharisees.
b. Read Mt 14:1–12. Summarize what happened to John the Baptist. Characterize Herod Antipas.

## Prayer Reflection

The most important prayer recited daily by Jesus and his Jewish contemporaries was the *Shema* ("Listen!"). It was a profession of faith in the one God. Christians can profit from frequent recitation of this powerful prayer, part of our rich spiritual heritage.

> Listen, Israel: Yahweh our God is the one, the only Yahweh. You must love Yahweh your God with all your heart, with all your soul, with all your strength. Let the words I enjoin on you today stay in your heart. You shall tell them to your children, and keep on telling them, when you are sitting at home, when you are out and about, when you are lying down and when you are standing up; you must fasten them on your hand as a sign and on your forehead as a headband; you must write them on the doorposts of your house and on your gates.
>
> — Deuteronomy 6:4–9

### reflection

Do you love God with all your heart, soul, and strength? If not, what is keeping you from doing so?

### resolution

The *Shema* instructs us to wear reminders of our faith in God and to post these words of faith on our homes. Examine your own home to see what visible evidences are present of your faith (for example, crucifixes, prominently displayed Bibles, religious art). If symbols of your faith are lacking, consider adding something to your bedroom wall that will remind you of your Christian belief.

*chapter* 3

# Introducing the Gospels

Traditional symbols for the four evangelists: Mark — the lion, Matthew — the man, Luke — the ox, John — the eagle.

This disciple is the one who vouches for these things and has written them down, and we know that his testimony is true.

There was much else that Jesus did; if it were written down in detail, I do not suppose the world itself would hold all the books that would be written.

— John 21:24–25

**In This Chapter**

**We will look at a method of studying the gospels that involves the following types of criticism:**

- **historical criticism**
- **source criticism**
- **form criticism**
- **redaction criticism**

One day a tired father came home from work only to be greeted by his energetic six-year-old son. All the father wanted was a few minutes of peace and quiet with a cold drink and his newspaper. To put his son off, he tore into small pieces a page of the newspaper he was reading. On one side was a large map of the world, on the other side a picture of a man. The father instructed his boy to put the map together again.

In a few minutes, the son returned to his dad with the map completed. Amazed, the father asked, "How did you do it so soon?"

"It was easy," replied the son. "All I did was put the man right. When I did that, the world came out okay, too."

This story pretty much sums up what Jesus came to do. His saving love has redeemed all people, has made them right with God. If we would live the new life Christ has given us, then we could literally change the world, transforming it with God's love.

The gospels announce the good news of what Jesus has done and, by the power of the Holy Spirit, continues to do for all of us. By putting together the story of Jesus in the gospels, we will also discover the meaning the gospel has for our world. Each evangelist provides a solid survey of the person and message of Jesus and his meaning for us. By studying how and why they wrote their gospels, we will read their accounts with more understanding and meaning.

## Changing the World by Changing Hearts

One theme that emerges consistently in the gospels is Jesus' attitude toward change. He gets at the root of what keeps us from being loving persons, asking us to turn our lives upside down. He challenges us to look at our life in an entirely new way.

Below are five challenging teachings from Matthew's gospel. Many of them are paradoxes, that is, apparent contradictions. They force us to take an honest look at ourselves and our commitment to Jesus. Look at these teachings, reflecting on their meaning. Rank yourself on a scale of 1 to 10 on each of them — 1 being a very weak commitment and 10 being very strong. Circle the appropriate number.

1. "Anyone who finds his life will lose it; anyone who loses his life for my sake will find it" (Mt 10:39). I frequently turn from temptation so I can be loyal to Jesus.

   1 2 3 4 5 6 7 8 9 10

2. "If anyone wants to be a follower of mine, let him renounce himself and take up his cross and follow me" (Mt 16:24). I willingly sacrifice some of my time, energy, and possessions for the welfare of others.

   1 2 3 4 5 6 7 8 9 10

3. "Many who are first will be last, and the last, first" (Mt 19:30). I think of pleasing parents, friends, and siblings before fulfilling my own desires.

   1 2 3 4 5 6 7 8 9 10

4. "The greatest among you must be your servant" (Mt 23:11). I'd rather help others than have others wait on me.

   1 2 3 4 5 6 7 8 9 10

5. "Anyone who raises himself up will be humbled, and anyone who humbles himself will be raised up" (Mt 23:12). I try not to brag. Rather, I try to show gratitude for all my talents, realizing they are gifts from God.

   1 2 3 4 5 6 7 8 9 10

## ▪ discuss ▪

1. Discuss other possible meanings for each of these sayings.
2. Come up with examples of people (famous or not) whom you believe exemplify each of these teachings.

3. Explain what would happen if students (and teachers!) in your school tried to live these sayings. Are they practical?
4. Find examples of advertisements that sell values opposite of those Jesus proposes.

**journal**

**Write about a time when you really tried to put one of these teachings into practice. Discuss the results. Was it difficult to do?**

## Critical Study of the Bible

Christians believe the Bible is the most important book ever written, a key source of divine revelation and a meeting point with God. It records God's action in human history, especially through the story of Jesus, God's Son. Reading it seriously and prayerfully can help us grow closer to God and to each other.

But how should we read it? Does the Bible mean whatever I think it means? Am I to take everything I read as the absolute, literal truth? How am I to understand what I read?

Not all Christians agree on the answers to these questions. Some people limit the Bible's meaning to their own personal interpretation. Others take a more *fundamentalist* view, which holds that everything in the Bible is completely factual — literally and historically true. On the other hand, some people believe that everything in the Bible is myth, that none of it is factually true. The Catholic position calls for a prayerful and critical interpretation of the Bible. We believe it is the inspired word of God, but that it requires a careful and studious reading to understand the literary forms, the symbolism, and the cultural factors that influenced it.

Today, many Protestant and Catholic scholars use several types of biblical criticism to study the New Testament. Criticism here is not a negative term; rather, it means looking carefully at the biblical texts in their historical and literary contexts — the customs and ways of thinking at the time the events took place and were written, and the forms in which the material was recorded. We will look at the following types: historical criticism, source criticism, form criticism, and redaction criticism.

*How Biblical Criticism Proceeds.* As we saw in Chapter 1, biblical criticism has identified three stages that led to the written gospels: 1) Jesus' historical life; 2) the period of oral tradition; and 3) the written gospels. The term *gospel* (good news) is common to all stages. This term refers to: 1) Jesus himself and what he came to proclaim — the coming of God's reign; 2) the preaching about Jesus — his victory over sin and death and our salvation; 3) the four officially approved written records of this good news — the gospels of Matthew, Mark, Luke, and John.

Careful, scholarly reading helps us to explore the meaning of a biblical passage by asking these kinds of questions:

1. What is the larger context surrounding this passage?
2. What religious, social, cultural, and historical realities influenced the writer?
3. What was the writer trying to say? What did he actually say? How did he say it?
4. How does what the writer wrote fit in with his larger work? with the rest of the New Testament? with the Old Testament?
5. For whom was this text being written? What was this audience like? What were its needs? How might the writer have adapted his materials to help this particular audience understand the gospel?
6. What literary device, if any, appears here? How do we normally interpret this kind of literary device? What does this passage mean, taking this device into consideration?

Scholars realize scripture study is a sacred science, the pursuit of knowledge about God and his dealings with us. Thus, they do their research prayerfully, seeking the guidance of the Holy Spirit who inspired the original texts. They approach their study in a spirit of humility, realizing that they are servants of God's word.

Through their collaboration with the pope, and the bishops teaching with him, Catholic scripture scholars contribute to the *magisterium*, the church's authoritative guidance for correctly understanding the meaning of sacred scripture. Jesus gave the church the power to teach in his name. He also promised that he would guide them in this teaching. Vatican II tells us:

> Since God speaks in sacred Scripture through men in human fashion, the interpreter of sacred Scripture, in order to see clearly what God wanted to communicate to us, should carefully investigate what meaning the

> sacred writers really intended, and what God wanted to manifest by means of their words.
>
> — Second Vatican Council
> *Dogmatic Constitution on Divine Revelation,* No. 12

**▪ *journal* ▪**

Read paragraphs 11 and 12 of the Vatican II document on revelation. Note the answer to the following questions.

1. How did God use the writers of scripture?
2. List three literary forms mentioned in the document.
3. Discuss one guideline the document says interpreters of scripture must follow in their work.

## Historical Criticism

Historical criticism asks: "What really took place behind this particular biblical text? What is the historical context?" This method of study uses dating techniques, archeology, and historical research to document and verify the biblical text.

For example, consider Jesus' parable of the sower. Here is Luke's version of it:

> "A sower went out to sow his seed. Now as he sowed, some fell on the edge of the path and was trampled on; and the birds of the air ate it up. Some seed fell on rock, and when it came up it withered away, having no moisture. Some seed fell in the middle of thorns and the thorns grew with it and choked it. And some seed fell into good soil and grew and produced its crop a hundredfold" (Lk 8:5–8).

You have probably heard this story many times. Has it ever struck you that the farmer in the story appears inept? His method of sowing seed seems careless, since so much of it falls on unfertile ground.

Historical research, however, tells us that farmers in Jesus' day sowed their seeds first and then plowed the ground. Today, farmers plow their fields first, thus turning under weeds and removing debris before planting their crop. Soil in Palestine was typically shallow and rocky. What initially seemed to be bad soil might end up being good soil after the *journal*

**Read Mt 4:12–17. Check a biblical dictionary and record in your journal four interesting, historical facts about Capernaum, an important city in Jesus' ministry.**

plowing. The reverse is also true; apparently good soil might end up being unproductive. The key point of the parable, though, is that some of the seed will eventually make it to good soil where its increase will be quite extraordinary.

This one detail about Palestinian farming techniques helps Jesus' parable come alive. Historical criticism helps us understand and appreciate every aspect of our study of the gospels and the New Testament.

## Source Criticism

Source critics are literary detectives whose job is to discover the source of the materials that the different evangelists used to construct their gospels. The most interesting work produced by New Testament scholars in this area deals with the way the similarities among the three synoptic gospels came about, the so-called "synoptic problem."

Matthew, Mark, and Luke are the synoptic gospels. When we line them up in parallel columns, we see many similarities among them. They can be "looked at together" (*syn*=together; *optic*=look). Note, for example, the following verses:

| Matthew 5:13 | Mark 9:49–50 | Luke 14:34–35 |
| --- | --- | --- |
| "You are salt for the earth. But if salt loses its taste, what can make it salty again? It is good for nothing, and can only be thrown out to be trampled under people's feet." | "Salt is a good thing, but if salt has become insipid, how can you make it salty again? Have salt in yourselves and be at peace with one another." | "Salt is a good thing. But if salt itself loses its taste, what can make it salty again? It is good for neither soil nor manure heap. People throw it away. Anyone who has ears for listening should listen!" |

The synoptic gospels have much in common and differ significantly from John. For example, Mark has 661 verses; 80 percent of these appear in Matthew while 65 percent appear in Luke. Matthew (1,068 verses) and Luke (1,149) are considerably longer than Mark, but they follow Mark's general outline in telling the order of events in Jesus' life.

Besides sharing some material from Mark, Matthew and Luke also have around 220 verses in common that do not appear in Mark. Furthermore, Matthew and Luke have material in each of their gospels that does not appear in any of the other three. These facts have prompted scholars to ask:

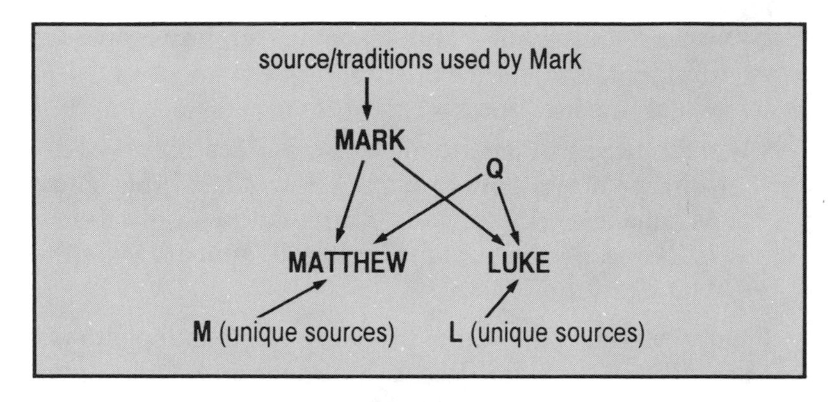


What sources did the evangelists of these gospels use when they composed their works?

There are many theories on the relationship between and among these three gospels. Some of these involve detailed and intricate arguments. The diagram here presents a commonly accepted, though simplified solution to the synoptic problem.

Most scholars accept that Mark invented the form of literature we know as a gospel, perhaps writing between 65 and 70, thirty-five to forty years after Jesus' death. The written gospel is a unique literary form. The gospels are not primarily biographies of Jesus, although they do contain biographical elements. The gospels are faith summaries that testify to the meaning of Jesus as the Lord and Savior. Their key purpose is to witness to Jesus, to instruct, and to inspire people to believe.

As far as we know, the author of Mark's gospel created this new literary device. He drew on the oral tradition he heard, the lived faith of his own community, and written sources available to him. For example, he may have referred to a list of Jesus' miracles to help jog his memory. Furthermore, a tradition based on a second-century bishop, Papias, holds that Mark was Peter's interpreter and that his gospel conveys many of the themes of Peter's own preaching.

Scholars further conclude that Luke and Matthew composed their gospels around fifteen years after Mark produced his. They hypothesize that Luke and Matthew had three different sources in front of them as they wrote:

1) Mark's gospel;
2) a common written source from which they got the 220 or so verses they have in common (Most of these

verses are sayings and teachings of Jesus; scholars designate this source **Q** after the German word *Quelle*, which means "source.");

3) their own independent sources. Matthew had a source known only to him. Scholars label this source **M**. Likewise, Luke had a source known only to him, **L**. None of this unique material appears in either Mark or John.

Finally, Matthew and Luke probably wrote independently of each other. In several places Matthew and Luke ignore certain key traditions recorded by the other. The most notable example is their two very different versions of the events surrounding Jesus' birth.

John's gospel differs a great deal from the synoptics. Written sometime in the 90s, it presents a very sophisticated theology of Jesus. Long discourses, or speeches, play a central role. Although the author of John's gospel was probably aware of the other three gospels, he does not draw on them. When you study John in greater detail, you will notice how unique it is.

■ *journal* ■

1. Carefully read Matthew and Luke's versions of Jesus' temptation in the desert (Mt 4:1–11; Lk 4:1–13). Answer the following questions:
   a. What details do Matthew and Luke share in common?
   b. What details does one offer that the other doesn't? Do you feel these are significant? Explain.
2. Compare Matthew and Luke's version of the Beatitudes (Mt 5:3–6, 11–12; Lk 6:20–23). Discuss the differences. Which do you prefer? Why?

## Form Criticism

Form critics have two jobs. First, they study small units of a text rather than the whole document in order to determine how each took shape in the period of oral tradition before the gospels took written form. Second, form critics identify the literary type or form used by the biblical author. For example, two literary forms found in the gospels are historical narrative and parable.

Each form has its own rules for composition. It also presents the truth in a different way. Parables, for example, are stories that challenge people to look at something in a new way. They are not accounts of real events. We read a parable like the good Samaritan primarily for its religious message (love everyone, including your enemies), not its historical accuracy. The accounts of the trial and death of Jesus, on the other hand, are historical narratives, telling what happened to Jesus at a definite time and place.

Below is a list of some of the different forms you will meet while studying the gospels.

| **Form** | **Definition** | **Example** |
|---|---|---|
| Miracle story: healing or exorcism | usually has these elements: introduction; request for help; Jesus' intervention; result; reaction | "And going into Peter's house Jesus found Peter's mother-in-law in bed and feverish. He touched her hand and the fever left her, and she got up and began to serve him" (Mt 8:14–15). |
| Miracle story: nature miracle | a powerful sign that shows Jesus' mastery over the elements | "Then he woke up and rebuked the wind and the rough water; and they subsided and it was calm again. He said to them, 'Where is your faith?'" (Lk 8:24–25). |
| Parable | a vivid short story told to convey religious truth | "The kingdom of Heaven is like the yeast a woman took and mixed in with three measure of flour till it was leavened all through" (Mt 13:33). |
| Hyperbole | a deliberately exaggerated saying to highlight the topic under discussion | "If your hand or foot should be your downfall, cut it off and throw it away" (Mt 18:8). |
| Hymn/prayer | used in early liturgies and incorporated into the gospels | "In the beginning was the Word:<br>the Word was with God<br>and the Word was God . . ." (Jn 1:1ff.). |

The gospels contain many other forms besides those listed here. There are examples of genealogies, prophetic sayings, instructions to disciples, legal sayings, predictions, proverbs, and the like. By recognizing and appreciating the forms we will be able to read the gospels much more intelligently.

---

### Form Criticism

Each of the passages below illustrates one of the forms discussed above. Match the name of the form with the passage. Be able to defend your choice in a discussion.

1. Mk 8:1–10 ____________
2. Lk 1:46–55 ____________
3. Mk 1:23–26 ____________
4. Lk 12:49____________
5. Lk 10:29–37 ____________

---

## Redaction Criticism

Redaction criticism focuses on the evangelists as editors: how and why they arranged their materials the way they did. ("To redact" means "to edit for publication.") The evangelists compiled and adapted their various sources into a unified work. Redaction critics try to discover the particular theological slant or insight of the given writer and how this influenced his arrangement of the material.

To get an accurate picture of Jesus in the New Testament we need to look at the various portraits painted by all the evangelists. But we must keep in mind two key insights: 1) Each wrote for a particular audience; 2) each had a particular theological theme he wished to underscore in his own presentation of the good news. Redaction criticism, then, helps us discover how the theology of each evangelist and the needs of his audience helped shape his final work.

Study the following chart to get an overview of the four gospels. Pay particular attention to the audience and the major theological theme of each evangelist.

| GOSPEL | Author | Date | Audience | Major Theological Themes |
|---|---|---|---|---|
| **Matthew** | Jewish-Christian scribe | 80s | Jewish-Christians | Jesus is the fulfillment of Judaic prophecies; he is the new Moses imparting the new Law of Love |
| **Mark** | perhaps John-Mark, missionary helper of Paul/ Peter | 65–70 | a suffering Christian community, perhaps in Rome | Jesus is the Suffering Servant Messiah; imitate Jesus' fidelity by not losing heart; the way to glory is through the cross |
| **Luke** | Gentile companion of Paul; a doctor; also wrote Acts | 80s | a Gentile-Christian church, perhaps in southern Greece | Jesus' salvation is open to everyone, especially the oppressed, poor, despised; Jesus is the universal savior |
| **John** | a disciple of the "beloved apostle," John | 90s | several Christian churches around the Roman Empire have been suggested — notably Ephesus, but also Antioch in Syria and Alexandria | most theologically sophisticated of all the gospels: Jesus is the eternal Word of God, God's Son who came as Bread for our eternal salvation; He is the Way, the Truth, and the Life |

*Doing Redaction Criticism.* To see how redaction criticism works, please read the stories of Jesus' birth in Matthew (chapters 1 and 2) and Luke (chapters 1 and 2). As you read through these accounts you will note several key differences. These suggest that Luke and Matthew are interested in theology rather than history.

Recall how the gospel was first preached: The early disciples announced the good news of Jesus' resurrection and glorification; they reviewed the deeds of his public life and the events of his passion and death; they joyfully proclaimed that Jesus' death and resurrection conquered sin and death. Those who hear the gospel should repent, believe the good news of salvation, receive the Holy Spirit, and be baptized into Christ's body.

Only after many years of proclaiming this basic message did the Christian community assemble the stories of Jesus' birth. These stories helped believers understand the full significance of Jesus' saving works and words. The symbolism of these stories reveals Jesus' identity, his purpose for coming into the world, his meaning for believers. By carefully studying what Matthew and Luke say about Jesus' birth, we can get an excellent overview of how their gospels will proceed.

*Matthew's Version.* Recall that Matthew was a Jewish-Christian writing for other Jewish-Christians. His purpose was to show that Jesus fulfilled Old Testament prophecies about the Messiah. He draws on themes from the Hebrew scriptures with which his audience would be very familiar. Here are some ways he does this.

1. Matthew traces Jesus' ancestry to Abraham, the father of the Jews. *Jesus is the promised Messiah,* greater than King David. He is the son of David, son of Abraham, the fulfillment of Jewish hopes.

2. Jesus comes to us *through the power of the Holy Spirit.* He is divine and human. He is to be named Immanuel, a name that means "God is with us." Isaiah prophesied his origin: *"Look! the virgin is with child and will give birth to a son whom they will call Immanuel"* (Mt 1:23).

Matthew also reports that another son of David, Joseph, accepts the angel's message about Jesus' divine origin.

3. *Jesus is born in Bethlehem,* David's home and the town Micah prophesied would be the home of the Messiah (see Mt 2:6). The magi — Gentiles — recognize him as a king when they present him the royal gifts of gold, frankincense, and myrrh. Here Matthew hints at the way the resurrected Lord would commission his apostles to preach the gospel to all nations (see Mt 28:19).

4. *Jesus is the new Moses. He is also the new Israel.* Matthew uses a specifically Jewish literary form known as *midrash,* which retells past scriptural events to help explain and interpret a present event. The intent is not to be historically

accurate so much as it is to convey theological and religious truth. For example, Herod's slaughter of the innocents is not documented in any historical record of the time. Matthew uses it to remind the reader of Moses' brush with death as an infant.

Joseph, the foster father of Jesus, brings to mind the Old Testament patriarch, Joseph, who saved his starving kinsmen by inviting them to Egypt. Joseph takes Mary and Jesus to Egypt to save Jesus from Herod. Jesus is the new Israel who leaves Egypt, according to the prophet Hosea: "*I called my son out of Egypt*" (Hos 11:1).

*Luke's Version.* Luke tried to show his Gentile-Christian audience that Jesus was the universal Messiah. Let's look at some of the details and patterns Luke includes in his gospel.

1. *He interweaves the stories of Jesus and John the Baptist to show that Jesus is the Messiah and that this Messiah has divine origins.* Mary, his mother, accepts the mystery of God's work

with humble faith. Her cousin Elizabeth recognizes the miracle that has taken place:

> "Of all women you are the most blessed, and blessed is the fruit of your womb. Why should I be honored with a visit from the mother of my Lord?" (Lk 1:42).

John's father, Zechariah, blesses God's wondrous work, saying to his son:

> "And you, little child,
> you shall be called Prophet of the Most High,
> for you will go before *the Lord*
> *to prepare a way for him*" (Lk 1:76).

The angels sing their song of praise to the Messiah, and the old prophets Simeon and Anna bless God for being allowed to see him.

2. *Jesus reveals himself first to the lowly.* Jesus was born in poverty. Shepherds are the first to see him. Because their occupation would not allow them to keep faithfully the religious rituals demanded by the Law, pious Jews such as the Pharisees looked down on them. Yet, Jesus came to such as these. He is the Messiah of the simple folk, the sinners, and the outcasts.

3. *Jerusalem plays a key role.* Luke, who also wrote Acts, sees Jerusalem as a key symbol in the Christian story. In his gospel, Luke shows Jesus on a journey to Jerusalem. In Jerusalem, Jesus' passion, death, and resurrection accomplish our salvation. In this city, too, the Holy Spirit descends on the apostles and sends them to the ends of the earth to proclaim Jesus as Lord.

Luke tells us that from the very beginning Jerusalem figures prominently in Jesus' story. As the gospel opens, Zechariah is in Jerusalem. After Jesus' birth, Joseph and Mary present him in the Temple. And at age twelve Jesus travels to Jerusalem for the Passover feast. His time there as a youth points to a future day when he will again confound the learned, some of whom will plot his death.

## ▪ focus questions ▪

1. How do fundamentalists read the Bible? Contrast their view with a Catholic view of studying the Bible.
2. How does biblical criticism approach the Bible?

3. What were the three stages in the formation of the gospels?
4. Discuss the three meanings of the term *gospel.*
5. What are some of the questions biblical criticism tries to answer?
6. What are some factors the Catholic scholar must take into consideration as he or she studies the Bible?
7. Read Luke 20:45–47. Give two examples of the types of questions the historical critic would ask of this text.
8. What does source criticism address?
9. What is the so-called synoptic problem? Outline an acceptable approach to it.
10. How can you explain that Matthew and Luke share some verses that do not appear in Mark? How do you explain that Luke has some verses that appear in neither Mark nor Matthew?
11. List, define, and give an example of five different literary forms found in the New Testament.
12. Define *redaction criticism.*
13. Do we have to take each detail of the infancy narratives as historically accurate? Explain. What is the value of these stories?
14. Discuss several ways the nativity narratives of Matthew and Luke differ. Explain why they differ.
15. Identify the major theological concern of each evangelist. Identify the audience for which each evangelist wrote.
16. Define the meaning of these terms:

| | |
|---|---|
| evangelist | *Q* |
| magisterium | synoptic gospels |
| midrash | |

## ▪ *vocabulary* ▪

**Look up these words and copy their definitions in your journal.**

**discourse**
**insipid**
**paradox**
**redact**

## ▪ *exercise* ▪

Let's continue our study of redaction criticism to see how Luke and Matthew adapted Jesus' teaching on prayer for their particular audiences.

First, carefully read Mt 6:5–15 and Lk 11:1–13. Then study the following outline:

| Matthew | Luke |
| --- | --- |
| 1. When you pray... | 1. Jesus himself prayed |
| 2. Don't be phony | 2. Show us how to pray |
| 3. Don't babble on; keep your prayers short | 3. Here's a formula: Our Father |
| 4. Here's an example of a short prayer: Our Father | 4. Parable of the friend — be persistent |
| 5. Pray with a forgiving heart | 5. Parable of the father: your prayer will be answered |

How do you explain these differences? How might Matthew and Luke have tailored Jesus' teaching to their particular audiences?

Matthew's Jewish-Christian audience had a rich tradition of prayer. Thus, he assumes they are already praying, but he wants them to keep their prayers short and to the point. They should also trust that God will indeed answer their prayers. Followers of Jesus should always be forgiving and not like some hypocrites of Jesus' day who showed off so others would think they were holy. This teaching on prayer would make a lot of sense to a Jewish convert who had accepted Jesus.

Luke, on the other hand, wrote for Gentile converts. As pagans, they did not have a heritage of prayer. Thus, Luke points to Jesus as one who often prayed (Jews would have known this). Luke also presents the Our Father as a formula of the perfect prayer, one in which we call God *Abba*. Luke is assuring his audience that Jesus' Father is loving and intimately concerned about his children. Pagans experienced their gods as often cruel and vindictive. Finally, Luke stresses the need to be persistent in prayer. He assures his audience that prayers *will* be answered. (Gentile-Christians needed this reminder because Gentiles did not have the Jewish experience of Yahweh who indeed answered the prayers of his special people.)

Respond to these questions in your journal.

1. Does Luke's or Matthew's teaching on prayer make more sense to you?

2. How do you define prayer? How do you pray? Are your prayers wordy? When do you pray? Where do you pray?
3. Is it important to pray? Why or why not?
4. Do you get discouraged when you pray? Do you need to be reminded or encouraged to pray often?

Discuss your responses with your classmates.

## Prayer Reflection

"Yes, if you forgive others their failings, your heavenly Father will forgive you yours; but if you do not forgive others, your Father will not forgive your failings either" (Mt 6:14–15).

### ▪ *reflection* ▪

When has someone's forgiveness really helped you grow?

### ▪ *resolution* ▪

Who needs your forgiveness? What can you do to show that you do indeed forgive this person? Will you do it?

*chapter* 4

# The Gospel of Mark

## Following the Suffering Messiah

"Anyone who wants to become great among you must be your servant, and anyone who wants to be first among you must be slave to all. For the Son of man himself came not to be served but to serve, and to give his life as a ransom for many."

— Mark 10:43–45

**In This Chapter**

**We will examine:**

- **authorship, date, audience, and outline of Mark's gospel**
- **key themes and passages in Mark**
- **Jesus preaches the good news**
- **the way of discipleship**
- **the paschal mystery**

Some people maintain that the apostles fabricated the Jesus story. But they have a difficult time trying to explain the heroism of these same early witnesses to the life, death, and resurrection of Jesus of Nazareth. The apostles and other early witnesses were insulted for their testimony about Jesus. Most of them were called to prove the sincerity of their beliefs by sacrificing their very lives for their Master.

Christian tradition holds the following: Matthew was slain with a sword in Ethiopia; Mark died at Alexandria, after being mercilessly dragged through the streets of that city; Luke was hung on an olive tree in Greece. John was put in a caldron of boiling water, but miraculously escaped death. He was exiled to the island of Patmos and died there an old man, the only apostle who did not meet martyrdom.

Peter was crucified at Rome in an inverted position. Paul, after various tortures, was beheaded by the bloodthirsty emperor Nero. James the Greater was beheaded by the Jewish leaders in Jerusalem. James the Lesser was thrown from a lofty pinnacle of the Temple and then beaten to death with a club.

Bartholomew was flayed alive, while Andrew was bound to a cross from which he preached to his tormentors until he died. Tradition holds that Thomas was run through with a lance in India; Jude was pierced with arrows; Matthias was stoned and then beheaded; Barnabas was stoned to death.

Jesus tells us that if we want to follow him we must pick up our crosses and be willing to die. Certainly these brave early Christians knew the cost of discipleship. Mark's gospel stresses the need to suffer for Jesus and the importance of being faithful in the midst of temptation and even persecution. The Jesus of Mark's gospel asks each of us: "Are you willing to be counted as one of my disciples? Are you willing to pay the price of bearing the name Christian?"

## Service and You

Reread the quote that opens this chapter. It states a key theme of Mark's gospel. Evaluate your own attitude toward service by checking any statements that apply to you.

1. Often we seem to ignore Jesus' call that we be servants because...

   ____ a. we claim it is not meant for us.

   ____ b. we pretend we don't know what it means.

   ____ c. we say that someday we will respond, but today we are too busy with other things.

   ____ d. we say it is not practical.

   ____ e. we say we'll start when others do.

2. I sometimes am reluctant to serve others because...

   ____ a. I'm afraid others might laugh at me.

   ____ b. I'm afraid others will think I'm foolish.

   ____ c. I'm afraid to be taken advantage of.

   ____ d. I'm not really sure what to do.

   ____ e. I don't think I have many skills to help others.

3. Reflect on those who are closest to you and state a concrete way you can serve each of the following:

   a. your parents: ____________

   b. a sibling: ____________

   c. a teacher: ____________

   d. a friend: ____________

   e. a classmate: ____________

   f. a fellow parishioner: ____________

### ▪ discuss ▪

1. Are people today eager or reluctant to serve others? Explain.
2. Which careers could you choose that would exemplify Christian service?

### ▪ journal ▪

Write several paragraphs telling about a time when you truly went out of your way to help others. Discuss the following factors:

a. why you decided to help
b. whether it was a difficult or easy experience
c. how others reacted to you
d. what you felt about yourself after the experience

Share these in class.

## Authorship, Date, Audience, and Outline of Mark's Gospel

*Who?* Mark's gospel does not reveal the identity of its author. Not until the second century or so was "The Gospel *According to Mark*" added to the text. However, many scholars identify the author of this gospel as the John Mark who appears in Acts and several other New Testament writings. John Mark was Paul's traveling companion and a relative of Barnabas.

Another clue to Mark's identity comes from the church historian Eusebius. He quotes the testimony of Papias, an early church father: "Mark, having become Peter's interpreter, wrote down accurately whatever he remembered of what was said or done by the Lord, however not in order."

*When? Why? Where?* Nero executed Peter in Rome around 64. One theory holds that Mark, Peter's interpreter, wrote his gospel shortly after this event to bolster the sagging faith of Christians who were suffering for their beliefs. According to this theory, Mark may have written the gospel as early as 65 or 66.

However, another hypothesis places the composition of Mark shortly after the destruction of the Jewish Temple in 70. It holds that Mark 13 is an actual description of the Temple's destruction, rather than a prediction of what would take place. Supporters of this view, drawing on a third-century church tradition, also suggest Mark might have been the founding father of the church in Alexandria. As a leading church figure, then, he might have written his gospel to encourage Christians in Syria and Palestine.

We cannot be certain when or where Mark's gospel was written or even who did the writing. However, we are very clear on why it was written: to encourage suffering Christians to remain faithful to their Lord who himself suffered and died for them.

*What? How?* Drawing on oral traditions (perhaps Peter's own testimony), written collections of the parables, miracle stories, and other sayings of Jesus, and an outline of Jesus' passion story, Mark masterfully weaves his materials into his gospel. Mark provides a simple geographical framework for presenting the *teaching of Jesus* (the good news of God's reign) and the *preaching about Jesus* (he himself is the good news). This framework includes Jesus' baptism in the Jordan (1:1–13), his preaching and performing miracles in Galilee (1:14—9:50), his journey to Jerusalem (10), and his preaching, rejection, crucifixion, and resurrection there (11:1—16:8). Matthew and Luke will adopt this general outline in their own versions of the good news.

**"No pain, no palm;
no thorns, no throne;
no gall, no glory;
no cross, no crown."
— William Penn**

Mark continually asks his readers two questions about Jesus: First, *"Who is this person?"* Mark shows that many of Jesus' contemporaries were not clear on Jesus' identity. Second, Mark asks, *"Will you follow Jesus?"* Mark's Jesus is the model of faith. The Christian must follow in his footsteps. The cost is high, but the reward is great.

*Outline of Mark.* Before reading Mark's gospel look at this simple but helpful overview. It sets up the gospel as a drama with two acts.

Prologue (1:1–13)

Act 1: Jesus preaches the good news (1:14—8:26).

A. the beginning of his ministry in Galilee: call of disciples, mighty works, controversies (1:14—3:6)
B. Jesus in his own territory (3:7—6:5)
C. his teaching on discipleship and his miracles meet misunderstanding (6:6—8:26)

Transition: Who is Jesus?
Messiah = Son of man = Suffering Servant (8:27–33)

Act 2: The way of discipleship is the way of the cross (8:31—16:8).

A. the Son of man is to suffer (8:31—10:52)
B. Jesus in Jerusalem (11:1—13:37)
C. Jesus' passion, death, and resurrection (14:1—16:8)

Second ending of Mark (16:9–20)

## Reading Mark

Mark is the shortest gospel. It is simply and briskly written. It also provides a basis for understanding both Matthew and Luke, the other synoptic gospels.

Read all of Mark's gospel. You can do it in around an hour. If you want to break your reading into two segments of a half-hour each, then first read to Mk 9:1 before taking a break. Read for the big picture. At this point, don't get bogged down in details.

**discuss**

**When you finish your reading, share with your classmates your favorite quote from Mark's gospel and why you like it.**

**journal**

a. Write out five favorite quotes or passages.
b. Note five passages that raise questions in your mind, passages you want to come back to for discussion or further study.

## Key Themes and Passages in Mark

*The Prelude (Mk 1:1–13).* Mark's opening verse — "The beginning of the gospel about Jesus Christ, the Son of God" — summarizes several main themes of his gospel. Jesus, the proclaimer of the gospel, is himself now proclaimed as the good news. Mark summarizes Jesus' preaching: "The time is fulfilled, and the kingdom of God is close at hand. Repent, and believe the gospel" (1:15). The reign Jesus came to announce and usher in is intimately related to Jesus himself.

A second major issue Mark addresses is the question of Jesus' identity. Mark tells us that the man Jesus is the Christ, the Messiah, the Son of God. From the opening verse there is no doubt who Jesus is. Readers of Mark have a distinct advantage over the gospel characters, including the apostles, who continually misinterpret and misunderstand Jesus.

*Jesus' Baptism and Testing in the Desert.* Mark and the other evangelists single out Jesus' baptism by John as the event that inaugurates his public ministry. John the Baptist, clothed in camel-skin, recalls the prophet Elijah who would come before the Messiah. Jesus' baptism once again unveils his identity. A dove, a symbol of the Spirit, descends on Jesus and a voice from heaven reveals, "You are my Son, the Beloved; my favor rests on you."

Mark ends his prologue with Jesus' forty-day retreat in the desert, recalling the Israelites' forty years in the desert. Satan tested him, but Jesus emerged triumphant. His mission is clear: to preach God's reign faithfully, even if it would lead to his death.

### ▪ journal ▪

Mark does not spell out for us the details of Jesus' desert temptation. Luke (4:1–13) and Matthew (4:1–11), however, list three temptations. Please read one of these accounts and answer the questions in your journal.

1. What is the nature of each temptation? In your judgment, which temptation is the most severe? Why?
2. What in each temptation might have appealed to Jesus?
3. What is Jesus' response to the temptations?

### ▪ discuss ▪

Temptations are related to real and perceived needs, for example, our need for affirmation, for acceptance by our peers, for gratification of basic drives such as hunger or sex.

1. What are three needs of today's teens? What are some corresponding temptations to these needs?
2. When are we most vulnerable to temptations? What can we do to resist them?

## Act 1: Jesus Preaches the Good News (1:14—8:30)

*A Teacher of Authority.* The first "act" of Mark's gospel raises the question of Jesus' identity: Who is this man? Mark tells us Jesus went to Capernaum and began to teach, but his teaching caused people to ask questions. It left a deep impression on his hearers because he "taught them with authority" (1:22). People recognized the power in his words because they rang true and because Jesus often backed up his words with action, with miracles.

For example, when Jesus cured the man possessed by an evil spirit, the people were *astonished* and began asking what it all meant. They said: "Here is a teaching that is new, and with authority behind it: he gives orders even to unclean spirits and they obey him" (1:27).

*Jesus the Miracle-Worker.* Jesus performs many miracles in Mark's gospel. They include: *healing miracles* (Peter's mother-in-law, a leper, a man with a withered hand, the woman who bled for twelve years, a deaf mute, and a blind man); *exorcisms* (the man in the synagogue in Capernaum and the raging possessed man in the Gentile territory of Gedara); *nature miracles* (calming the storm, walking on water, and feeding over five thousand people); *raising people from the dead* (Jairus' daughter).

These miracles are intimately related to Jesus' proclamation of the reign of God. Take, for example, the story of Jesus curing the paralytic (2:1–12). This miracle illustrates the miracle form.

1. *An introduction* presents the case. In this situation, the room in which Jesus is teaching is so crowded that the friends of the paralyzed man lower him through the roof.

2. A display of *faith* leads to Jesus telling the man that his sins are forgiven. This particular miracle story involves Jesus in a controversy with his opponents. Forgiving the man's sins angers some scribes sitting nearby because every Jew knew that only God could forgive sin. They thought that Jesus must be blaspheming. Jesus said to them:

> "Why do you have these thoughts in your hearts?. . .But to prove to you that the Son of man has authority to forgive sins on earth" — he said to the paralytic — "I order you: get up, pick up your stretcher, and go off home" (Mk 2:8–10).

3. Jesus' cure is the third dimension of the typical miracle — his *response to the person in need.*

4. The *result* of the miracle follows. In this case, the man got up, picked up his stretcher, and walked.

5. The final aspect of most miracle stories is the *reaction* to Jesus' deed: "They were all astonished and praised God saying, 'We have never seen anything like this'" (2:12).

The miracles of Jesus played an extremely important role in his ministry. The Greek word *dynamis* (compare the English word *dynamic*) is the word the synoptic gospels use for "miracle." *Dynamis* means power. Through the miracle accounts Mark shows that the power of God has broken into human history. The nature miracles show that Jesus has mastery over creation; the exorcisms disclose Jesus' power over evil; the raisings of the dead reveal Jesus' power over death; his many cures prove that God's power is healing the human condition right now. Salvation is taking place through Jesus; the power of God's reign is revealed in their very midst.

Miracles are also *signs*. They illustrate important themes in Jesus' message. For example, Jesus has the power to forgive sin, the source of our alienation from God and others. He proved this dramatically in the healing we studied above. Forgiving sin and backing up his words with a healing is a convincing sign that Jesus is God's Son, because only God can forgive sin. Feeding 4,000 people with seven loaves of bread (Mk 8:1–10) symbolically points to Jesus as the source of our life, the sign of God's presence in our midst. He is the living bread who sustains and nourishes us.

Faith plays a major role in Jesus' miracles. On two occasions in Mark (5:34 and 10:52) and one in Luke (17:19), Jesus says, "Your faith has saved you." On other occasions, miracles lead to faith. For example, after Jesus cured the demon-possessed man in Gentile territory, the man wanted to follow Jesus.

Mark also tells us what the lack of faith can do, even in Jesus' home town of Nazareth: "He could work no miracle there, except that he cured a few sick people by laying his hands on them. He was amazed at their lack of faith" (6:5–6). His own friends and neighbors would not believe that Jesus was God's Messiah, the agent of God's reign.

Jesus' miracles call for faith in him and in the reign of God. Recall the theme of Jesus' preaching, "Repent, and believe the good news." Repentance — turning away from sin — and faith in Jesus are intimately united.

---

## Miracles

Read the miracle of Jesus calming the storm (Mk 4:35–41). Outline below the five elements of this story.

1. Introduction: ______________________________

2. Faith: ______________________________

3. Response: ____________________
4. Result: ____________________
5. Reaction: ____________________

■ *discuss* ■

1. Did the apostles have faith? Explain.
2. Why did Jesus perform this particular miracle? What does it communicate about God's power? What does it symbolize?
3. What is Mark trying to teach Christians by means of this miracle?
4. Do you believe miracles happen today? Do you see any signs of God's action in your life? Do you see any demonstrations of his power in the world? Explain.

---

*The Human Jesus.* Mark presents the most vivid portrait of the human Jesus. In Mark's gospel, Jesus is a warm, loving person. He embraces the children who come to him (9:36). He looks with love on the rich young man, even though the young man cannot bring himself to sell all he has to follow Jesus (10:21). Jesus' many miracles prove his deep compassion for those who suffer. For example, he responded to the plea of the father of the epileptic son (9:23–28) and to the cry from Bartimaeus, the blind beggar (10:46–52).

Jesus is also angry on several occasions, for example when the disciples bar the children from approaching him (10:14) and when the apostles repeatedly fail to grasp his message, as they do when he tells the parable of the sower (4:13). He also professes ignorance about the exact time of the world's end (13:32), and curses a fig tree for its failure to bear fruit, even though it is not the season for figs (Mk 11:12–14).

Mark reports all reactions of Jesus, even when they seem to show Jesus in a bad light. The most remarkable case is the opinion of his own relatives: "They set out to take charge of him; they said, 'He is out of his mind'" (Mk 3:21). Matthew and Luke drop this incident from their gospels.

*Jesus: The Messiah.* Mark's gospel leaves no doubt that Jesus is the Messiah, but he fulfills this role in a way that even his closest disciples cannot fathom. For the first half of his ministry, Jesus's actions and words met with confusion, amazement, and misunderstanding. People of the time expected their messiah to be a king, a military leader, someone who would deliver them from Rome's political oppression. Because Jesus saw the role of the Messiah in a different light, and because he wanted people to approach him with faith and as a Servant-Messiah, he shunned publicity and kept his identity a secret.

**reading scripture**

**Read these passages from Mark's gospel: 1:21–28, 32–34, 40–45; 3:7–12; 5:21–43; 7:31–37; 8:22–23. How do these passages show us that Jesus wanted to keep his identity a secret?**

Halfway through Mark's gospel (8:27–33), this question of identity begins to be resolved. One day, on the road to Caesarea Philippi, Jesus asked his disciples:

> "Who do people say I am?" And they told him, "John the Baptist, others Elijah, others again, one of the prophets." "But you," he asked them, "who do you say I am?" Peter spoke up and said to him, "You are the Christ." And he gave them strict orders not to tell anyone about him (8:27–30).

Note that many of his contemporaries recognized him as a special person — a prophet, or Elijah who was to precede the true Messiah, or John the Baptist come back to life. Peter, however, professes Jesus' true identity: He is the Messiah! Jesus accepts the title, but once again instructs his disciples not to make it known to everyone.

Jesus' concept of the Messiah differs radically from popular expectation. Even Peter, the leader of the apostles, found it difficult to accept the significance of Jesus' true identity:

> Then he began to teach them that the Son of man was destined to suffer grievously, and to be rejected by the elders and the chief priests and the scribes, and to be put to death, and after three days to rise again; and he said all this quite openly. Then, taking him aside, Peter tried to rebuke him. But, turning and seeing his disciples, he rebuked Peter and said to him, "Get behind me, Satan! You are thinking not as God thinks, but as human beings do" (8:31–33).

The secret of Mark's gospel is revealed: Jesus is the Suffering Servant prophesied by Isaiah centuries before. He is surely the Messiah, but with a cross, not a glittering throne. He will walk the rocky path to Calvary, not the marble floors of a Jerusalem palace. When Jesus refers to Peter as Satan he makes it very clear that even his closest disciples are tempting him to walk the wrong path.

## Jesus and You

"Who do *you* say that I am?" Check off the appropriate description.

Jesus, for me, is...

____ a friend

____ my Savior

____ a teacher

____ a nice guy, but that's all

____ my Lord

____ the Son of God

____ a misguided prophet

____ the greatest person who ever lived

____ someone I turn to for help

____ not much of anything

____ my hero

____ ______________________
(write your own)

I am, for Jesus...

____ a friend

____ unreliable

____ a helper

____ someone he can count on

____ a person of faith

____ a prayerful person

____ not much yet, but I will be one day

____ his greatest fan

____ someone who tries to see him in others

____ growing in knowledge of him

____ ______________________
(write your own)

### journal

Respond to Jesus' question. Tell him who you think he is and why you have that opinion of him.

## Act 2: The Way of Discipleship (8:31—16:8)

*Suffering Service — Call to Discipleship.* Soon after Peter proclaims Jesus' true identity, Jesus begins a series of three predictions of what will happen to him. He also instructs his followers that, if they wish to be his disciples, they will have to follow in his footsteps.

After the first prediction of his passion, death, and resurrection, Jesus says:

> "If anyone wants to be a follower of mine, let him renounce himself and take up his cross and follow me. Anyone who wants to save his life will lose it; but anyone who loses his life for my sake, and for the sake of the gospel, will save it" (Mk 8:34–35).

The message to the audience for whom Mark wrote is clear: *The followers of Jesus must be prepared to suffer as Jesus himself suffered.* When Christians try to live their convictions in an unconvinced world, they must be ready to follow Jesus' way.

Jesus repeats his message two more times (9:32 and 10:33–34), but once again the apostles misunderstand him. They argue over who is the greatest among them, but Jesus instructs them that the sign of greatness is service to others (9:33–37). To be open to the reign of God means to accept it without cunning or guile: "Anyone who does not welcome the kingdom of God like a little child will never enter it" (10:15). On another occasion, James and John ask for places of honor in Jesus' kingdom, but Jesus tells them that he can only promise them suffering (10:35–40).

People in Mark's audience were being martyred for their belief in Jesus, and betrayal and denial were real temptations. Mark continually encourages his audience and his readers to be faithful to Jesus. Being faithful means being willing to suffer for him.

---

### Suffering Servant

Read Isaiah 52:13—53:12, the Fourth Suffering Servant Song. These verses were written to encourage the exiled Israelites in Babylon with the message that redemption comes through suffering.

Jesus applied these verses to himself. He was the Messiah who was also the Suffering Servant. The Son of man would die so all people could have superabundant life.

**journal**

Note five points from these verses that apply to Jesus. (Check footnotes or other references in your Bible for help.)

**discuss**

**Share a time when you suffered for your faith in Jesus.**

*The Son of Man.* Although Mark's Jesus accepts the titles *Messiah* and *Son of David* (referring to the promise made to King David that a descendent of his would sit on Israel's throne as the promised Messiah), *Son of man* is Mark's favorite title for Jesus. In fact, it is Jesus' favorite self-designation in all the gospels — appearing fourteen times in Mark, thirty times in Matthew, twenty-five times in Luke, and thirteen times in John.

The scriptural background to this title reveals two different things. First, it was used to contrast the poverty and weakness of human beings to God's might and power (see Is 51:12 or Ps 8:4). In using the title, then, Jesus emphasized his identification with our ordinary human nature. When we hear Jesus proclaim: "Then they will see the Son of man coming in the clouds with great power and glory" (Mk 13:26), however, he echoes Daniel 7:13 and other sacred Jewish writings that refer to the Son of man as a supernatural figure. Jesus ushers in the fullness of God's reign and he will serve as the judge of all humanity.

*Transfiguration (9:2–8).* Chapter 9 of Mark's gospel opens with the dazzling unveiling of Jesus' true identity. Here Peter, James, and John get a glimpse of Jesus' future glory. God dramatically reveals to them that Jesus, the Son of man, is really divine: "This is my Son, the Beloved. Listen to him" (9:7). However, once again, Jesus warned the three privileged eyewitnesses not to reveal what they had seen "until after the Son of man had risen from the dead" (9:9).

## The Paschal Mystery (14:1—15:47)

The term *paschal mystery* refers to the passion, death, and resurrection of Jesus, the saving events that have won eternal life for us. Our baptism initiates us into the paschal mystery; the eucharist re-enacts and celebrates it. The paschal mystery, the heart of our faith in Jesus, is the climax of Mark's gospel.

Many scholars conclude that the first thirteen chapters of this gospel are primarily an introduction to the story of the passion. The passion stories were probably the oldest ones circulating in the Christian communities. The four gospels agree on the essentials, but each evangelist has his own way of telling the story. Mark's gospel emphasizes the way everyone abandoned Jesus at the end: Judas betrays him; the three disciples fall asleep during Jesus' agony; Peter denies knowing him; when Jesus is arrested, everyone flees — even the young man who runs away naked leaving his sleeping garment behind, a detail found only in Mark. The Jewish and Roman authorities harshly judge Jesus. The soldiers and later the people mock him. The only words Jesus cries from the cross — *"My God, my God, why have your forsaken me?"* — seem to show that Jesus thought even God had abandoned him, making a mockery of his life.

Mark shows that to be a follower of Jesus means to follow in the master's path of suffering and abandonment. But Mark ends with good news. The centurion, whom Mark uses to represent all Christians, acknowledges who Jesus truly is: the Son of God. And God accepts the total surrender of his Son by bringing him back to a life full of glory. What God has accomplished for the Son will be the gift he gives to us, too, if we walk with Jesus.

Let us turn now to sketch Jesus' last hours. Please check the texts and read the explanatory notes provided.

The Upper Room of the Last Supper. The building was much reconstructed by the Franciscans in the fourteenth century and has a definite Gothic style.

1. *Conspiracy against Jesus* (14:1–2). The leaders plot Jesus' death in a way that would not cause an uprising. They feared that the crowds might try to rescue him.

2. *Woman anoints Jesus at Bethany* (14:3–9). This anointing foreshadows Jesus' death. Recall that *Christ* means "anointed one." This woman of simple faith recognized Jesus' true identity and mission when so many others did not.

3. *Judas' betrayal* (14:10–11). Judas' avarice compels him to turn Jesus over to the chief priests for money.

4. *Preparations for Passover Supper* (14:12–16). Mark hints at the impending doom, telling us that this was the day the Passover lambs were slaughtered. The man carrying the water jar would have been an unusual sight since this was

normally a woman's work. The disciples would have easily recognized him. Note that Jesus is planning the Passover meal, thus showing that he is in control. The sacrifice of his life for us is a free act of his will.

5. *Last Supper* (14:17–25). Jesus once again foretells his betrayal, and once again the apostles are confused. Jesus shares his last hours with his friends at a Passover meal, the Jewish feast that celebrates Yahweh delivering them from Egypt. The paschal mystery is God's new covenant with us, his new way of delivering his people. At every eucharist Jesus comes to us under the forms of bread and wine and reminds us to pour ourselves out in service to others.

6. *Gethsemane* (14:26–52). Jesus makes three predictions: 1) the disciples will scatter when he dies; 2) he will precede them to Galilee after his resurrection; 3) Peter will deny him. Then Mark turns to the vivid picture of Jesus' agony. It reveals to us that the human Jesus did not want to die. Like all people, he feared death. But from the depths of his soul, he prayed the perfect prayer: that Abba's will be done. Jesus courageously accepts his destiny and does not flee.

The apostles cannot stay awake. Judas betrays Jesus with a kiss, a sign of friendship. The arrest takes place at night, in darkness, the realm of Satan. Significantly, Jesus repudiates the use of force, thus rejecting the expectation of many (especially the Zealots) that the Messiah would be a political leader.

7. *Before the Sanhedrin* (14:53–72). The so-called trial of Jesus has stumped lawyers for centuries. It was contrary to Jewish law to hold trials at night. The false witnesses cannot agree on their testimony. Jesus does not defend himself because he knows that it would be useless against trumped-up charges. But forcefully and without hesitation he does acknowledge that he is the Christ, the Son of the Living God. And he predicts that the Son of man will come in glory. This claim outraged the leaders. They accused Jesus of blasphemy and began to spit on, strike, and ridicule him.

Peter, who had earlier acknowledged Jesus' true identity as Messiah, now denies knowing his friend and Master. But he realizes what he does and bursts into tears of sorrow and repentance. In the end Peter remained faithful to Jesus until his own death on a cross.

8. *Jesus and Pilate* (15:1–20). Under Roman occupation, only Roman authorities had the power to crucify capital

offenders, so the Sanhedrin had to fabricate a crime deserving the death penalty under Roman law. They cleverly accuse Jesus of sedition, of claiming to be a king in competition with Caesar, a capital offense. Pilate knows Jesus is innocent, that "it was out of jealousy that the chief priests had handed Jesus over" (v. 10). He schemes to escape responsibility by invoking a custom of freeing a criminal during the high feast. But his plan backfires. The mob, stirred up by the chief priests, calls for a known murderer, Barabbas. Pilate feels his hands are tied. Thus, he mercilessly scourges Jesus and then turns him over to the soldiers for crucifixion. Pilate mockingly calls Jesus "king of the Jews," not knowing that Jesus is indeed king of the Jews, of all people, of the universe. Pilate's soldiers continue to mock Jesus, dressing him in a purple gown and crowning him with thorns. They insult him and spit on him in utter contempt.

9. *The Crucifixion* (15:21–47). Jesus is so weakened by the beatings that he needs the help of a passer-by, Simon of Cyrene, to carry his cross.

Jesus is nailed to the cross. Crucifixion was a cruel method of torture, bringing a horrible death by dehydration and respiratory arrest.

Crucified between two bandits, Jesus is taunted by passers-by who dare him to save himself. But, as he did in the desert, Jesus resists any temptation to save himself alone. He remains faithful to the end.

Jesus' last words are *"My God, my God, why have you forsaken me?"* (*"Eloi, eloi, lama sabachthani?"*) Observers mistakenly think he is calling on Elijah for help, not recognizing that he is quoting Psalm 22. Shortly afterward, Jesus lets out a loud cry and dies.

Mark tells us that the veil in the Temple's sanctuary is rent in two, symbolizing that Jesus' death begins a new age when all people can worship God directly, in truth and justice. Jesus has removed the barrier separating us from God.

Jesus' death brings from the Gentile centurion a profound profession of faith: "In truth this man was Son of God" (v. 39).

The true disciples of Jesus included some women who remained with him to the end. Joseph of Arimathea, a member of the Sanhedrin but also a disciple of Jesus, asks for permission to bury him. Before releasing the body, however,

Pilate makes sure that Jesus is dead. Mark tells us Jesus' death came after six hours on the cross.

10. *Resurrection* (16:1–8; 9–20). Mark's gospel ends quickly. He reports that the women go to the tomb and meet a young man in a white robe who tells them that Jesus is risen. He instructs the women to tell the disciples and Peter to meet Jesus in Galilee. But, out of fear, the women flee and say nothing to anyone.

Scholars say that Mark's original gospel ended at verse 8 and that later editors added verses 9–20. These other verses report some of the appearances reported by the other gospels: to Mary Magdalene, to two disciples outside the city, to the apostles in Jerusalem.

Some suggest that Mark ended his gospel at verse 8 to invite readers to substitute themselves for the women at the empty tomb. The women were too frightened to spread the word. Consequently, Mark's readers are responsible for spreading the good news of Jesus' resurrection. In a sense, Mark is saying, "This gospel has been written for you. Imitate Jesus. Go and spread his word through your actions."

## ▪ journal ▪

1. Would you have denied knowing Jesus? Explain.
2. Write Jesus' obituary in two hundred words or less.
3. Which character in the Passion narrative do you most identify with? Why?
4. What does Jesus' death mean to you?

Share and discuss your responses to these questions.

## ▪ focus questions ▪

1. Who was the probable author of Mark's gospel?
2. State one of the theories about the place and time of the composition of Mark's gospel.
3. Why was the gospel of Mark written?
4. What is the geographical framework Mark uses in his gospel?
5. What is the one-verse summary Mark provides of Jesus' preaching about the reign of God?
6. What does the opening verse of Mark's gospel reveal about Jesus?

7. In what way did Jesus teach "with authority"?
8. What is the typical framework of a gospel miracle story? Outline any miracle from Mark's gospel according to this framework.
9. The gospels look on miracles as *power signs*. Apply both of these aspects of miracle — power and sign — to Jesus' curing of the crippled man (Mk 2:1–12).
10. Discuss some examples of Mark's portrait of the human Jesus.
11. Discuss Jesus' identity as the Messiah.
12. Based on Jesus' exchange with Peter on the road to Caesarea Philippi, what was probably Jesus' greatest temptation throughout his public ministry?
13. Explain the meaning of these titles of Jesus: *Christ*, *Suffering Servant*, and *Son of David*.
14. Explain why Jesus may have chosen the title *Son of man* as his favorite self-designation.
15. Mention four places in Mark's gospel where Jesus is revealed as the *Son of God*.
16. What is the price Mark's Jesus asks us to pay to be his disciples?
17. To what does the term *paschal mystery* refer?
18. Outline the key events of the passion narrative. Comment on how Mark shows the utter abandonment of Jesus at the end.
19. Why might Mark have ended his gospel at 16:8?

**■ vocabulary ■**

**Copy the meaning of these words into your journal.**

**taunt**

**Transfiguration**

## ■ journal ■

1. Please read either Matthew's (26—27) or Luke's (22—23) version of the passion and death of Jesus. List in your journal at least five differences between Mark's version and either Matthew's or Luke's.
2. Consult a biblical dictionary to research how crucifixion took place in the Roman world.

---

## Prayer Reflection

For the next several chapters, your prayer reflection will ask you to engage in *imaginative prayer*. The imagination is one of our most active mental faculties. It enables us to picture and enter into many different scenes. It can help us picture what is possible and then work to try to achieve that ideal.

It is easy to pray imaginatively with the gospels. Here's how to do it.

1. Calm down. Find a restful prayer position. Breathe slowly and deeply. Let the cares of the day drain from you.
2. Next, enter into the presence of the Lord. Imagine Jesus next to you assuring you of his love. Look at his features: his clothing, the length and color of his hair, his complexion, his smile, his eyes. Feel him putting his arm around you.
3. Now pick up a gospel passage. Put yourself and Jesus into the passage. For example, make yourself a character in the story. Use all your senses — sight, smell, touch, taste, hearing. Listen carefully to the words of the passage. Pause often and let them sink in. But let your imagination flow with the picture.
4. Then reflect. Return to the present. Ask the Lord to show you what the passage might be saying to you.
5. Then thank the Lord for the time he spent with you. Take a resolution from your prayer time and try to put it into practice.

Try this technique right now with the passage of the storm at sea (Mk 4:35–41). Enter the scene as one of the apostles. Use all your senses. Then hear Jesus speaking to you.

## ▪ reflection ▪

What are you afraid of right now? What is buffeting you about? Have you asked the Lord to help? Have you heard his reply, "Be calm"?

## ▪ resolution ▪

Begin each day of the coming week asking the Lord to take control of any of the storms you might face during the day. When tough times come, return to the image of your friend and Savior, Jesus, calming the storm.

*chapter* 5

# The Gospel of Matthew

## Teaching the Christian Life

Church on the Mount of the Beatitudes, Galilee.

"You are light for the world. A city built on a hill-top cannot be hidden. No one lights a lamp to put it under a tub; they put it on the lamp-stand where it shines for everyone in the house. In the same way your light must shine in people's sight, so that, seeing your good works, they may give praise to your Father in heaven."

— Matthew 5:14–16

### In This Chapter

We will look at:

- authorship, date, audience, and outline of Matthew's gospel
- key themes and passages in Matthew's gospel
  - — Sermon on the Mount
  - — missionary discourse
  - — parables of the reign of God
  - — advice to the church
  - — final judgment

Many baseball analysts list Hall-of-Famer Ted Williams of the Boston Red Sox as one of the very best all-time hitters. Although endowed with good eyesight and natural talent, Ted believed that many other people had these same two gifts. What made him different was his desire to excel and some good old-fashioned hard work. According to him, hitters are made, not born.

Acknowledging that he could always hit, Williams credits his willingness to spend countless hours mastering his craft as his secret to success. For example, he was the first kid at school every morning waiting for the janitor to open up the athletic storage area so he could grab the bat. Fierce determination to excel fired him. But wishful thinking was not enough to find Ted Williams a place in baseball history. Working hard to be his personal best accomplished for Ted Williams what talent could never achieve on its own.

In the Sermon on the Mount, Jesus teaches, "So be perfect, just as your heavenly Father is perfect" (Mt 5:48, NAB). This high ideal is the standard Jesus sets for those of us who bear his name. Followers of Jesus have the talent to excel in living the Christian life. The gifts of the Holy Spirit give us the ability to follow Jesus faithfully.

But to achieve perfection in following, we have to work at developing our skills. Matthew's gospel presents a teaching Jesus, one who gives much advice on how we can and should live the Christian life.

## The Beatitudes

Memorize the Beatitudes (Mt 5:3–10). Check your living of the Christian life using the following scale:

1 — I am making very good progress on this
2 — I am average on this
3 — I have a long way to go

| Beatitude | Rating | Statement |
| --- | --- | --- |
| How blessed are the poor in spirit: the kingdom of Heaven is theirs. | ____ | I know that without God, I am nothing. I recognize my need for and dependency on him. He is my all. |
| Blessed are *the gentle: they shall have the earth as inheritance.* | ____ | I am mannerly toward others, respecting their worth as individuals. I cherish everything in God's creation. |
| Blessed are those who mourn: they shall be comforted. | ____ | I have the ability to empathize with others. I can feel for those who are hurting and can show that I care. |
| Blessed are those who hunger and thirst for uprightness: they shall have their fill. | ____ | Doing God's will of living an upright life is my #1 priority. It outranks popularity, success, and material possessions. |
| Blessed are the merciful: they shall have mercy shown them. | ____ | I not only pity those who are troubled, but I do something to help. I am a compassionate person. |
| Blessed are the pure in heart: they shall see God. | ____ | I am a person of integrity. "What you see is what you get" in my case. I am honest in all my dealings with others. |
| Blessed are the peacemakers: they shall be recognized as children of God. | ____ | I can deal with my own anger in constructive ways. I can help smooth tense situations among others. I am a person of peace. |
| Blessed are those who are persecuted in the cause of uprightness: the kingdom of Heaven is theirs. | ____ | I am willing to suffer ridicule for my beliefs. Jesus can count on me. |

## ▪ *journal* ▪

Jesus ends the Beatitudes with this message to his followers:

> "Blessed are you when people abuse you and persecute you and speak all kinds of calumny against you falsely on my account. Rejoice and be glad, for your reward will be great in heaven; this is how they persecuted the prophets before you" (Mt 5:11–12).

Write about a time when you were abused because of your Christian convictions. Did this make you a better or worse person? Explain. Share with your classmates.

■ *discuss* ■

**List three examples of how a teen can live each of the Beatitudes.**

## Authorship, Date, Audience, and Outline of Matthew's Gospel

*Who?* Church tradition dating from the time of Papias (c. 130) tells us that the apostle Matthew (or Levi, the tax collector) wrote down the sayings of Jesus in Aramaic around 40–45. This original collection, called the Hebrew gospel, if it ever existed, has been lost. The author of Matthew's gospel as we know it is anonymous. An apostle and a direct eyewitness to the historical Jesus would probably not have borrowed so heavily from Mark's gospel. The author of Matthew might have known the apostle Matthew or used a source of sayings in Aramaic, in addition to the material he borrowed from Mark.

■ *discuss* ■

Many scholars believe the author of Matthew's gospel was a former Jewish scribe. They believe that Mt 13:52 — "every scribe who becomes a disciple of the kingdom of Heaven is like a householder who brings out from his storeroom new things as well as old" — is autobiographical. To further support this view, compare Mk 14:43 with Mt 26:47. Discuss these two questions:

1. What detail did Matthew leave out in recounting the arrest of Jesus?
2. Can you explain why he might have done so?

*When? Where?* Because Matthew borrows heavily from Mark's gospel, it had to be written after Mark. Matthew's gospel also is clearly aware of the destruction of the Temple in 70. Furthermore, scholars believe Matthew, more than any other gospel, shows many signs of the antagonism between early Jewish-Christian communities and the Jews who survived the First Revolt.

During the 80s, Christian Jews were driven out of the synagogues. This naturally resulted in strained relations, a tension reflected in Matthew's gospel, which contains many sharp sayings directed against the Pharisees. For example, in Matthew 23 Jesus repeatedly rebukes the Pharisees for their shortcomings.

Matthew's gospel was probably written sometime between 70 and 90, most likely in the 80s. The probable location of writing was in Palestine or Syria, perhaps in Antioch, and, like all the gospels, the original was written in Greek.

*Why? What? How?* Of all the gospels, Matthew's was clearly written for Jewish-Christian communities. The Jewish customs, Matthew's manner of speaking, his reference to Hebrew prophecies, and the gospel's themes suggest this.

Matthew assumes that his audience is familiar with Jewish customs. For example, he uses terms like Preparation Day and talks about the ritual washing of hands before eating and the wearing of phylacteries. (A *phylactery* was a small leather capsule that was fastened on the forehead or on the upper left arm so that it hung at the level of the heart. It contained miniature scrolls with four passages from the Jewish Law, all alluding to the need to keep God's Law before one's eyes and heart. Pious Jewish males would wear these all day once they reached adulthood.) In none of these cases does he explain his terms.

Matthew also uses Hebrew terms such as *Gehenna* (the Jewish term for hell) and *Beelzebul* (a Hebrew term for the devil). He writes "kingdom of Heaven" rather than "kingdom of God" because Jews believed God's name was too sacred to pronounce.

The author of Matthew draws on his rich familiarity with the Hebrew scriptures to show how Jesus' life and teaching fulfill God's promises to Israel through Moses and the prophets. Matthew wanted his readers, who revered Jewish Law, to know that Jesus is the new lawgiver, the new Moses: "Do not imagine that I have come to abolish the Law or the Prophets. I have come not to abolish but to complete them" (Mt 5:17).

Several themes in Matthew's gospel underscore his purpose for writing and the audience for whom he intended it. Although Matthew's is the most Jewish of the gospels, presenting Jesus as the fulfillment of Hebrew prophecy, it reminds its readers that Jesus commanded his early disciples to spread the gospel to all the nations (see Mt 28:16–20). Christians who had been Jews and were now rejected by

■ *journal* ■

**Here are several Old Testament prophecies the author of Matthew uses to show how Jesus is the promised one. Read five of them and note how Jesus fulfills them.**

| | |
|---|---|
| 1:22–23 | 8:17 |
| 2:18 | 21:4–5 |
| 2:5–6 | 12:16–21 |
| 2:23 | 21:42 |
| 2:15 | 13:35 |
| 4:14–16 | 27:9 |

their synagogues needed to be told that they should not look too longingly to the past. Jesus is for all people everywhere.

Judgment is another major theme in Matthew's gospel. For example, several parables deal directly with the second coming of Christ and the theme of the last judgment. Some of the Christians for whom Matthew wrote may have been discouraged that the Lord had not yet returned in his full glory. Matthew had to remind his readers that we should always stand in readiness for Jesus because we do not know the hour when he will return.

Matthew has a great interest in the church. It is the only gospel where the word for church (*ekklesia*) appears (see Mt 16:18 and 18:17). He sees the church as the community of Christ's disciples who must carry on his work.

Matthew's gospel collects Jesus' teachings for Christian instruction — both for new converts but also for Christians who are struggling to deepen their life in Christ. We can look on Matthew almost as a catechism, an instruction manual for Christian life and teachings. Matthew became the most popular of all the gospels in the early church. Its organization, summaries of Jesus' teaching, adaptability for public worship, references to the Hebrew scriptures, and inclusion of most of Mark and much of Luke quickly made it the most useful of all the gospels for church life.

*Outline of Matthew.* Scholars have proposed many different outlines for Matthew's gospel. A traditional view suggests that Matthew organized his gospel into five major sections to suggest a comparison to the first five books of the Old Testament (the Pentateuch). According to this explanation, Matthew wanted to compare Jesus to Moses (traditionally believed to be the author of the Pentateuch).

Another view suggests that Matthew arranged his gospel into five sections of instructions. Each section has a narrative that tells us about Jesus' activities, and a major speech or discourse that gives Jesus' teaching. Each section ends with a familiar pattern, "Jesus had now finished what he wanted to say..." (7:28, 11:1, 13:53, 19:1, 26:1). This arrangement suggests that Matthew wanted to emphasize Jesus' role as teacher.

Matthew gives Jesus' answers to questions of vital concern to new Christians and to those who want to follow Jesus more closely: "What is the Christian life like? How should a

Christian leader act? What is God doing in the world? How should we, as Christians, act?"

The best way to look at Matthew's gospel, then, is to see it as a book of Christian instruction and administration. In the material that follows, we will focus on the five discourses of Jesus.

| | Chapters |
|---|---|
| *Prologue*: Birth of the Messiah | 1—2 |
| 1. *The New Law* | |
| Narrative: Jesus' Galilean ministry | 3—4 |
| Discourse: Sermon on the Mount | 5—7 |
| 2. *Christian Discipleship* | |
| Narrative: Ten miracles | 8—9 |
| Discourse: Mission of the Twelve | 10 |
| 3. *Reign of God* | |
| Narrative: Jesus and his opponents | 11—12 |
| Discourse: Parables of the kingdom | 13 |
| 4. *The Church: First-Fruits of God's Reign* | |
| Narrative: Messiah, the Shepherd of Israel | 14—17 |
| Discourse: Advice to the church | 18 |
| 5. *Judgment* | |
| Narrative: Controversies in Jerusalem | 19—23 |
| Discourse: The Second Coming and Judgment Day | 24—25 |
| *Epilogue*: Death and Resurrection of Jesus | 26—28 |

---

## Reading Matthew

Divide the class into five groups. Each group should read one of the narrative sections from the outline. Prepare a short oral report providing the following information:

1. the major events in this section
2. key characters

These reports should be delivered as the class studies each of the major discourses below.

---

# Key Themes and Passages in Matthew's Gospel

*Theme 1 — Christian Living: Sermon on the Mount (Mt 5—7).* The Sermon on the Mount is the best known and most important of the five discourses in Matthew's gospel. Jesus speaks with God's own authority and shows the way to true righteousness.

In the Sermon on the Mount, the author of Matthew collects many of Jesus' key teachings on Christian living. It is unlikely that Jesus delivered all of these at one place and in one time. We should understand the sermon as a classic example of a *didache*, that is, teaching directed to Christians who have accepted the gospel. It stresses that our belief in Jesus must translate into action: "It is not anyone who says to me, 'Lord, Lord,' who will enter the kingdom of Heaven, but the person who does the will of my Father in heaven" (7:21).

In this beautiful and challenging sermon, Jesus marks the path of true discipleship — true interior conversion that results in changed behavior. This conversion goes far beyond the minimal demands of the Law. Let us turn now to some key verses of this important discourse.

1. *Salt of the earth and light of the world (5:13–16).* After introducing the Beatitudes, Matthew gives us the images of Christians as salt and light. He wants his readers to know that if they live the Beatitudes — positive, loving responses to God and others — they will make a significant difference in the world. Salt flavors foods; so, too, the world should be a better place because Christians are in it. Salt also is used as a preservative; it saves meat for future consumption. Our presence as followers of Jesus should bring the world closer to eternal salvation.

Christians are also like light. Light dispels darkness. It shows the way. Our good works should be like a beacon of light that leads others to God. People need to see the good news in action in our lives.

2. *New standard of law (5:17–48).* Jesus tells us that he has come not to abolish the Law and the Prophets, but to fulfill them. He has come to fulfill all the promises of the old covenant. He amplifies six examples from the Law to drive home the importance of a changed heart, an interior attitude of love of God and neighbor. Note how Jesus underscores the point that mere external observance of the Law is not enough.

This section of the Sermon on the Mount contains two of Jesus' most difficult teachings: love of one's enemy and the injunction not to seek revenge. The Mosaic Law introduced strict justice into the legal system of its day — "an eye for an eye and a tooth for a tooth" — that is, justice should exact a precisely matched revenge. But Jesus tells us more is expected of Christians. We should forgive our enemies, break the chain of violence, and not seek revenge. Why? Because everyone is our brother or sister, everyone is our neighbor, even our enemies.

Christians have been struggling to live Jesus' new law for centuries. He sets high standards for his followers. From a human point of view, Jesus seems to be demanding the impossible. He calls us to stretch our attitudes toward the world, to be more loving and responsive to others. What is impossible for us to achieve on our own efforts is possible when we surrender to God's love and allow God to reign in our lives.

▪ *discuss* ▪

**Please read John 18:19–23. How did Jesus react to violence? Discuss how we should interpret his teachings in the Sermon on the Mount.**

## Living the New Law

Prayerfully read Matthew 5:21–48. Then examine your current status before Jesus' new law of love. Mark the place on the scale where you are right now. **1** means you are making excellent progress; **5** means you have a long way to go.

**Anger**: Do I easily and properly deal with anger, not letting it fester inside of me?

1 ____ 2 ____ 3 ____ 4 ____ 5

**Sexuality**: Do I respect my own sexuality and that of others, for example, by exercising self-discipline in thought and action?

1 ____ 2 ____ 3 ____ 4 ____ 5

**Oaths**: Am I a person of my word? Can I be counted on to always tell the truth?

1 ____ 2 ____ 3 ____ 4 ____ 5

**Forgiveness**: Do I truly forgive those who have harmed me, turning the other cheek rather than seeking revenge?

1 ____ 2 ____ 3 ____ 4 ____ 5

**Enemies**: Do I go out of my way to be courteous and even loving to people I do not like?

1 ____ 2 ____ 3 ____ 4 ____ 5

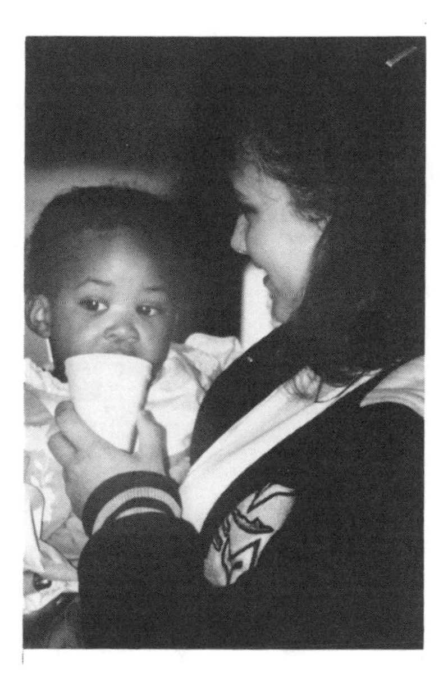

3. *Have a right attitude (6:1–34).* Chapter 6 of the sermon tells us that intention is critically important to Jesus. For example, Jesus wants us to examine our attitudes when we perform virtuous works. Is our motive to seek the approval of others? Or is it to give glory to God? Jesus tells us that his way to holiness is the path of quiet love. For example, when we give money to the poor, we should do it in a way that does not draw attention to ourselves. When we pray, we should do so simply and sincerely. The Lord's Prayer is the model prayer for Christians. When we fast, we should do so without calling attention to ourselves. God loves us with an everlasting love and has already rewarded us. Why should we be motivated by what others think?

Jesus tells us to trust his Father. Put first things first. If God takes care of the birds in the sky and the flowers of the field how much more will he watch over us, his children. Worrying about tomorrow is empty and leads nowhere. If we make doing God's will our top priority, then he will lead us and provide what we truly need.

4. *Requirements for Christian living (7:1–27).* The last chapter of the sermon reminds us that disciples of Jesus should not judge others. Just as God will forgive us as we forgive others, so he will judge us as we judge others. Thinking ourselves better than others, making them live up to our idea of what is holy, is arrogant. Jesus wants humility and gentleness in his followers. He teaches the golden rule: "So always treat others as you would like them to treat you" (7:12).

Jesus instructs us always to trust God, especially when we pray. God knows what is good for us, and if we ask for it, he will grant it. He warns us about false prophets, perhaps a problem in the community for whom Matthew wrote. But even today, many false prophets vie for our attention, making false promises of happiness. Jesus says we can judge a tree by its fruits. Check out the lives of the people making promises. Are they credible? Are they loving? Do they bring joy, peace, true happiness? In short, Jesus warns us to avoid bad fruits.

The sermon concludes by encouraging us to take Jesus' words to heart and build our lives on them. It is not enough to mouth them; we must *put them into action!* These teachings are a solid foundation for a Christian life, a foundation that nothing can shake.

## Applying the Sermon on the Mount

*What? — Me Worry?* Jesus tells us not to worry. Here are some issues that concern young people today. Rank these from the one that most concerns you **(1)** to the one that least concerns you **(10)**.

____ making and keeping friends

____ grades

____ getting a good job

____ your relationship with God

____ whether people like and accept you the way you are

____ having enough spending money

____ getting into a good college

____ your relationship with someone of the opposite sex

____ your looks

____ acquiring possessions

### ▪ discuss ▪

a. What does it mean to worry? Has worrying ever helped you? Explain.

b. What does Jesus mean when he says not to worry? Is his advice practical?

### ▪ journal ▪

Jesus tells us to live our lives in the present, seeking to do God's will in everything. Analyze a typical school day. Write how your life would change if you took his advice — Don't worry about anything except loving God and other people. Would you survive the day? Would it be worth trying?

*Theme 2: Missionary Instructions (Mt 10).* Jesus commissions his apostles to do as he did — cure the sick, raise the dead, cleanse those suffering from skin diseases, exorcise devils (10:8). Matthew tells us that after naming the twelve apostles, Jesus instructed them to proclaim the gospel to the Jewish people, avoiding contact with Gentiles. In Matthew's account, Jesus concentrated his earthly ministry on proclaiming the reign of God to the Chosen People; after his resurrection, the church would take the message to all people.

Jesus wants his apostles to proclaim the gospel in a spirit of poverty, not burdening themselves with accumulating money or carrying excess baggage. They should receive the hospitality of anyone who offers it.

It is certainly a privilege to work with and for Jesus, but part of the price of discipleship is the cross. Matthew makes it very clear that not everyone will accept the gospel: "I am sending you out like sheep among wolves; so be cunning as snakes and yet innocent as doves" (10:16). The travails Matthew describes might be the very ones his community was actually suffering. Leaders question and scourge them;

**discuss**

**How can your faith cause discomfort in your life?**

betrayals take place; false accusations are hurled at them; persecutions are widespread. But Jesus promises two things: 1) The Spirit will be there to help the disciples stand firm and testify courageously to the truth of the gospel; 2) the loving Father, who has counted every hair on their heads, will watch over them with love and tenderness.

Jesus praises anyone who testifies to others about him. In turn, Jesus will stand up for Christians before his Father in heaven. Jesus warns, though, if we proclaim that we belong to him, division will take place. He calls for decision. . . right now:

> "No one who prefers father or mother to me is worthy of me. No one who prefers son or daughter to me is worthy of me. Anyone who does not take his cross and follow in my footsteps is not worthy of me. Anyone who finds his life will lose it; anyone who loses his life for my sake will find it" (10:37–39).

Jesus uses strong imagery when he says he has come to bring a sword to the earth. Jesus, the Prince of Peace, is not advocating violence here. Rather, he uses a vivid image to illustrate the truth that if we choose Jesus as our first priority we will encounter resistance and will need to overcome it.

Matthew directs Jesus' missionary discourse not only to the apostles, but also to his own community and to Christians of all time. Proclaiming Jesus in word and deed is indeed a privilege, but to bear Christ's name also means we will suffer for him. Speaking for Jesus enables him to live in us: "Anyone who welcomes you welcomes me; and anyone who welcomes me welcomes the one who sent me" (10:40).

*Theme 3: The Reign of God (Mt 13).* Matthew reports seven parables Jesus used to teach about the reign of God. Parables are *short stories drawn from ordinary life that make a comparison with a religious message.* The parable of the mustard seed, for example, teaches that God's reign starts very small; however, in time, it will grow very large. As the birds will find shelter in the mustard tree, so will God's reign provide refuge for all people.

The parables of the treasure and the pearl teach that one should sacrifice everything for the reign of God. Gaining entrance to the reign of God brings untold joy.

In the parables of the darnel and the dragnet, Jesus says that in this life it is not always clear who has chosen the reign of God and who has not. However, when history is over, there will be a time of judgment when God will separate the good from the wicked.

Often, the gospel writer added a further explanation of the parable that made a more complex comparison that applied to his audience. In the parable of the sower, for example, seeds sown by a farmer land on the footpath, on rocky or thorny ground, and on good soil. The seed on good ground thrives, yielding a large crop at harvest time. In the same way, the reign of God will triumph, despite what may happen in the meantime.

Matthew turned this parable into an allegory (a sustained comparison in which several elements of the story correspond to realities outside the story). He applied the kinds of ground to the various kinds of Christians in his community. His goal was to encourage his audience to be faithful to the word of God and make it bear fruit in their own lives. Here is an outline of the allegorical interpretation Matthew gives:

| | |
|---|---|
| the sower | someone who preaches/teaches the word of God |
| the seed | the word of God |
| seed on the path | people who hear the word of God but make no effort to understand it; the devil tempts them away from God's word |
| seed on rocky ground | people who embrace the word joyfully at first; but they are superficial and the slightest temptation causes them to give up |
| seed in thorns | people who embraced the word, but a love of riches and worries about daily living strangle their commitment |
| seed on good soil | Christians who hear, understand, and live the word of God. |

Matthew intends his community, and us, to strive to be like this last group of Christians. We should hear the word of God, understand it, and put it into practice.

## Interpreting Parables

1. Write a one-sentence interpretation of the parable of the yeast (Mt 13:33):

   ____________________

2. Outline the allegory of the parable of the darnel (weeds in the wheat, Mt 13:36–43). Treat these elements:

   sower of the good seed ____________________

   the field ____________________

   the good seed ____________________

   the weeds/darnel ____________________

   sower of the weeds ____________________

   harvest ____________________

   reapers ____________________

The meaning of the parable as allegory: ____________________

____________________

### ▪ discuss ▪

Reread the parable of the darnel (13:24–30), this time focusing on only one point of comparison. If the emphasis is at the end, what point might Jesus be making about the reign of God?

*Theme 4: Life in the Church (Mt 18).* The concepts of the reign of God and Christian discipleship are closely related in Matthew's gospel. Called "the gospel of the church," it collects several key sayings about how church leaders should conduct themselves. Jesus is present to his church, ruling it, guiding it, and using it to help him set up the reign of God. Nevertheless, Christians, being human, need constant reminders to overcome their sinfulness and to live as worthy members of God's church. Matthew realizes the intimate connection between the church and the reign of God, but he also knows that God's reign is greater than the church. The reign of God will come in its fullest glory only at the end of time.

In the meantime, Chapter 18 gives some very practical advice on how Christians, especially church leaders, should conduct themselves. Their task is to help God's reign come alive in the midst of their communities.

— The model of how power and authority are exercised in the church derives from Jesus, not from earthly authorities. "The one who makes himself as little as this little child is the greatest in the kingdom of Heaven" (18:4).
— Scandal (bad example) is a serious failing for Christian leaders. Christians must live holy and humble lives, giving good example to all.
— A true leader will go to extremes, like the good shepherd, to save the straying one. Church leaders should imitate Jesus' loving service even though this path might lead to suffering and death.
— Christians should try to settle community disputes among themselves, always seeking the good of the whole community and of one another. The mark of true reconciliation is forgiving brothers and sisters who have harmed us.
— Christian leaders should heed well the message of the parable of the unforgiving debtor. God will be stern with those who fail to forgive their brothers and sisters from their hearts.

Finally, Jesus assures Christians in all ages of the power of prayer in a community.

> "In truth I tell you once again, if two of you on earth agree to ask anything at all, it will be granted to you by my Father in heaven. For where two or three meet in my name, I am there among them" (18:19–20).

---

## The Church

Chapter 18 of Matthew gives us several guidelines on what the church should be and how it should reach out to others. Here are some more New Testament passages on the church. Please do the following:

- Read the references given. Note in your journal what is said about the church.
- Rate your own parish or school community to see if it lives up to the description of the church given. Mark according to this scale: + if the description fits; – if it does not fit; ? if you are not sure.
- Discuss the questions that follow.

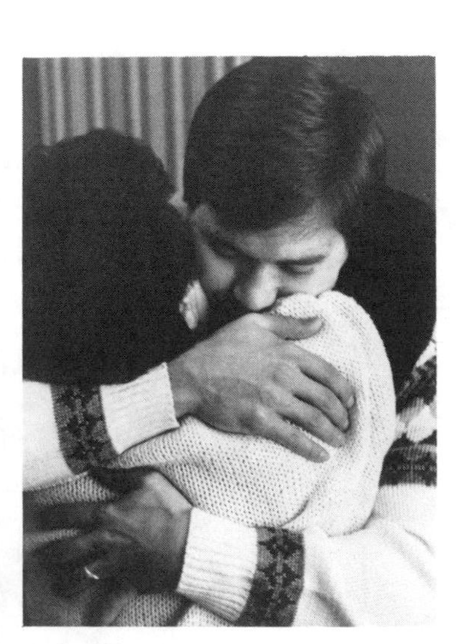

____ 1. a community that reaches out to other people (Mt 28:19–20)

____ 2. a community of believers (Rom 12:4–8)

____ 3. a forgiving community (Lk 19:10)

____ 4. a community founded by Christ on Peter and the apostles (Mt 16:15–19)

____ 5. a loving community (Mt 25:31–46)

____ 6. a eucharistic community (1 Cor 10:15–17)

____ 7. a community willing to suffer (Mt 5:10–12)

____ 8. a community of faith as taught by the apostles (Acts 4:1–4, 33)

## ▪ discuss ▪

1. Does the church have the right to excommunicate notorious sinners? (See Mt 18:15–18.) What actions do you think cut a person off from the church?
2. What standards should the church have for membership? How would Jesus answer this question?
3. How forgiving should Catholic schools be of wayward students? In light of Matthew 18, compose disciplinary guidelines for three serious offenses that could be committed by students at your school.

## ▪ journal ▪

Read Luke's version of the parable of the lost sheep, Luke 15:3–7. Answer these questions.

1. How do the audiences to whom Matthew and Luke address their parables differ?

2. What purpose did Matthew have in mind in telling his version of the parable? What purpose did Luke have?
3. Why do you suppose Luke adds the scene of the shepherd gathering his friends to rejoice?

---

*Theme 5: Judgment (Mt 24—25).* Jesus' final discourse deals with the end of the Temple, the end of the world, and divine judgment. By the time Matthew was writing, the Temple had been destroyed. The early church was still expecting Jesus to return soon. When this did not happen, they had to struggle with the words of Jesus that had given them this impression.

Matthew, like Mark before him, draws on the highly symbolic language of the book of Daniel to describe the coming of the Son of man. But he warns that because no one knows the exact day or hour, they should always be prepared for the Lord's return. Matthew drives home this point by relating a series of Jesus' parables on readiness: We should not be caught unaware like the contemporaries of Noah at the time of the flood; the master will return when we least expect it; Christians should be like the five wise virgins who were ready for the bridegroom's return.

The parable of the talents teaches that we should make good use of the time the Lord has given us. God has endowed us with gifts and a life to develop them. If we don't use what God has given us, we will have wasted our lives and be cast "into the darkness outside."

*Judgment (25:31–46).* The last discourse of Jesus concludes with the famous parable of judgment at the end of time. The Son of man will appear in the role of shepherd (v. 32), Lord (v. 37), and king (v. 40) to separate the sheep from the goats. The good will receive their reward, the wicked their punishment.

On what basis will the Lord judge us? His criterion is this: "In so far as you did this to one of the least of these brothers of mine, you did it to me" (25:40). Jesus identifies himself with the person in need. He will recognize us if we recognize him in the faces of those around us. But it is not enough to see the Lord, we must respond to him. Our eternal destiny hinges on whether we feed the hungry, give drink to the thirsty, clothe the naked, visit the sick and imprisoned.

*Conclusion.* Jesus' final teaching in Matthew challenges us to action. All of the teachings in Matthew's gospel outline the steps a true disciple must take to follow Jesus. The Sermon on the Mount (Mt 5—7) tells us that our actions flow from a transformed heart. Christians should strive for perfection in imitation of the Father. We should always do to others what we would want them to do to us. The missionary discourse (Mt 10) reminds us that if we accept Jesus and his gospel then we must share his good news with others, even though this might bring us rejection.

The reign of God discourse (Mt 13) reassures us that work for the reign of God will bring results, even if they are not apparent at first. The reward is untold joy. The discourse on the church (Mt 18) outlines the superior standards Christians must always exemplify in their work.

Finally, the judgment discourse (Mt 23—24) teaches that Christianity is something immensely practical. We must always strive to live loving lives *today*. We don't know when God will call us home or when the Son of man will return. Our chance to love is right now.

The opportunities to love are many. The poor, the needy, the hurting, the lonely, the victims of injustice — the Lord waits in all of these people for us to respond. If we do, then we are his people and he will call us "to eternal life." If we don't, the Master will say, "Go away from me" (Mt 25:41).

## Service

Service of others, especially the needy, is not optional for Christians. Either as a class or in small groups, undertake a project that will put into action one of Jesus' calls to love: feeding the hungry. Study the issue first, then devise and carry out a strategy. Here are some ideas.

### suggested procedure

1. *Study the issue.* Who are the hungry in your parish, neighborhood, or city? What is already being done to help them? Why are these people hungry? What is keeping them hungry?

2. *Decide what you can do to help.* Consider both a solution to the immediate problem and a long-term solution.
3. *Follow through on what you plan.* Assign jobs and set up a time-table. Let others know what you are doing and why. Enlist their support and help.
4. *Evaluate* — the process, the outcome, and your feelings about what you did.

## ▪ some ideas ▪

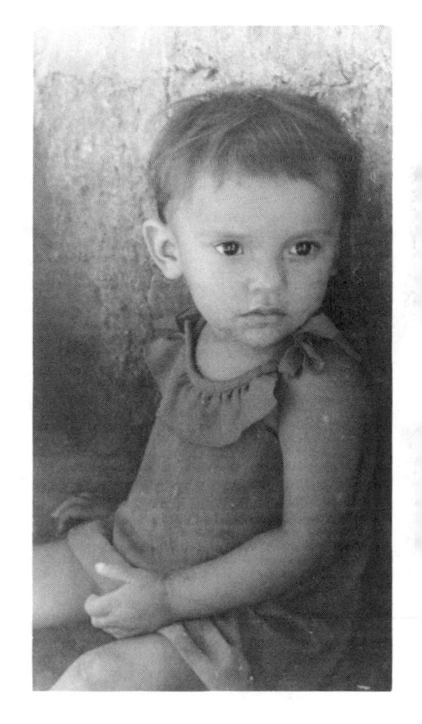

- agree to serve on a regular basis at a center or parish that serves meals to the needy
- sponsor a car wash or some other event to raise money to support a hunger center
- sponsor a "fast day" at school to empathize with the poor and make others aware of hunger
- sponsor a "hunger day" at school; suggest that students and faculty give up junk food and donate the cost to a hunger-relief agency; have an information component to the day — posters with hunger-awareness facts, guest speakers, films, etc.
- celebrate a eucharist, selecting appropriate themes from Matthew's gospel; when the gifts are offered, bring to the altar food that you bought with your own funds or some other symbol of your commitment to help the hungry; pray for the needy
- sponsor a campaign to help eradicate the waste of food in your school cafeteria

## ▪ focus questions ▪

1. Recite the Beatitudes from memory. What does each mean?
2. Identify the author of Matthew's gospel.
3. Give a probable date and place for the composition of Matthew's gospel.
4. Discuss several examples that show the *Jewish*-Christian flavor of Matthew's gospel.

5. Cite three Old Testament prophecies the author of Matthew believes Jesus fulfilled.
6. Matthew became the most popular of all the four gospels in the early church. Discuss two reasons why this was the case.
7. Give one explanation for the fivefold division in Matthew's gospel. After studying the gospel, what do you think?
8. In what way is a Christian light and salt?
9. What was Jesus' attitude to the Law? Discuss several examples of how he fulfilled it.
10. Jesus tells us not to worry. What does he mean?
11. What is the golden rule?
12. Discuss several requirements for Christian missionaries.
13. Considering Jesus' teaching, discuss this proposition: If your Christian faith is not costing you something, then you probably aren't living it.
14. What is a parable? Apply the meaning of the following parables to Jesus' message about the reign of God: the mustard seed, the sower, and the treasure in the field.
15. Discuss three bits of practical advice Matthew's gospel passes on to church leaders.
16. According to Matthew's Jesus, how should you be living your life today? How will God judge us at the end of time?

## vocabulary

**Copy the meaning of these words into your journal.**

**allegory**
**calumny**
**darnel**
**scandal**
**travail**

## exercises

1. List your three strongest talents. How can you use them in a practical way to serve others?
2. Read Matthew 23, a scathing criticism of the Pharisees. List five practices Christians should avoid. In another column, list positive practices that are opposite to what Jesus so harshly condemns.

## Prayer Reflection

For this biblical meditation, recall the steps outlined in the last chapter.

1. Assume a comfortable position. Relax and get ready for your time with the Lord.
2. Put yourself in the presence of the Lord. Feel his love surround you.
3. Turn to Mt 25:31–46. Put yourself into this last judgment scene. Engage all your senses. What do you see? Hear? Taste? Smell? Feel? The Lord is separating the sheep from the goats. Listen carefully once again to his words.
4. Reflect by reviewing your life right now. What if you were to die tonight at midnight? What could you say to the Lord?
5. Thank the Lord for his time with you.

> "Come, you whom my Father has blessed, take as your heritage the kingdom prepared for you since the foundation of the world. For I was hungry and you gave me food, I was thirsty and you gave me drink, I was a stranger and you made me welcome, lacking clothes and you clothed me, sick and you visited me, in prison and you came to see me."
>
> — Matthew 25:34–36

## ▪ reflection ▪

Who in your life needs your love right now?

## ▪ resolution ▪

What are you going to do to respond to this person. Be specific and be sure to follow through.

*chapter* 6

# The Gospel of Luke

## Joy and Salvation for All

"There will be more rejoicing in heaven over one sinner repenting than over ninety-nine upright people who have no need of repentance."

— Luke 15:7

**In This Chapter**

We will study:

- authorship, date, audience, and outline of Luke
- themes in the gospel of Luke
  - the role of the Holy Spirit
  - the power of prayer in Jesus' ministry
- the parables of Jesus

One day a newly baptized Christian approached his parish priest and asked, "How can God forgive sinners? Isn't God disgusted with people's hate, cruelty, greediness, and over-indulgence?"

The priest looked kindly on his friend and remarked, "Wasn't your grandfather a master furniture-crafter? And didn't your father take up the same trade?"

"Yes," replied the faith-filled convert.

"Well," continued the priest, "would your grandfather or father discard a table they were working on if it had a scratch on it?"

"Of course not," the young man answered. "A small scratch is hardly noticeable and can usually be polished away. It doesn't change the quality or value of the furniture or the craftsmanship of the carvers."

"A good answer," the priest replied. "It's the same way with God. He continues to find great value in his human creations despite their flaws. He'll never stop working with them, or forgiving them. As the poster says so well, God doesn't make junk."[1]

The gospel of Luke emphasizes the good news of God's salvation for everyone, joyfully proclaiming that God loves and forgives sinners.

## Priorities

Many people have said that one of the major problems of our day is *consumerism*, which induces us to buy products we don't need. Consumerism contradicts the values of Jesus, who taught us to make God's will our top priority and to live simply.

[1] Adapted from a story by William R. White in *Stories for the Journey* (Minneapolis: Augsburg Publishing House, 1988), p. 56.

How do you measure up to the values of Jesus? How much has the consumer culture captured your attention? In Luke's gospel, Jesus had much to say about our attitude toward money and possessions. Here are some of his sayings. Use this scale to judge your attitudes: **SA** (strongly agree), **A** (agree), **D** (disagree), **SD** (strongly disagree), **DK** (don't know).

____ 1. "How blessed are you who are poor: the kingdom of God is yours" (6:20).

____ 2. "Give to everyone who asks you, and do not ask for your property back from someone who takes it" (6:30).

____ 3. "Give, and there will be gifts for you: a full measure, pressed down, shaken together, and overflowing, will be poured into your lap; because the standard you use will be the standard used for you" (6:38).

____ 4. "Watch, and be on your guard against avarice of any kind, for life does not consist in possessions, even when someone has more than he needs" (12:15).

____ 5. "None of you can be my disciple without giving up all that he owns" (14:33).

____ 6. "No servant can be the slave of two masters: he will either hate the first and love the second, or be attached to the first and despise the second. You cannot be the slave both of God and of money" (16:13).

## journal

**Write a one-page reflection on what the "good life" is for you. Keep your essay in mind as you read the selections in Luke's gospel.**

## discuss

1. Check the context for the sayings given above. What do you think Jesus means for each of them?
2. In Luke 6:20, is Jesus praising poverty as such or "spiritual poverty"? What is the difference between the two?
3. Watch TV or listen to the radio for an hour; then analyze the advertisements:
   a. How do the commercials appeal to pleasure, the "good life," comfort, or status?
   b. Do the ads create false needs or do they appeal to real needs?
   c. What kind of people do the commercials depict? Comment.

# Authorship, Date, Audience, and Outline of Luke

*Who?* Early church fathers held that a Gentile Christian named Luke was the author of the third gospel. The author of Luke also wrote a history of early Christianity, the Acts of the Apostles. The style, language, and organization of Luke's gospel and Acts are so similar that we can only conclude they came from the same pen.

When reading Acts, we discover four passages (Acts 16:10–17, 20:5–15, 21:1–18, and 27:1—28:16) in which the narrative shifts from third person (*they* and *he*) to first person (*we*). Scholars conclude that the author of the work was present during the events described. Therefore, Luke was Paul's companion during some of Paul's missionary adventures.

The church historian Eusebius reports that Luke came from Antioch in Syria. An ancient tradition also holds that Luke was an artist and may have even painted a portrait of Mary. This is probably legend, but Luke was indeed a word artist, writing beautiful, polished Greek.

*When? Where?* We can deduce that Luke wrote for Gentile Christian communities. One of Luke's major themes, for example, is that the gospel is not for Jews alone but for everyone. Gentiles don't have to convert to Judaism to accept Jesus. Luke also eliminated passages that might confuse a non-Jewish audience, for example, the traditions of the Jews (see Mk 7:1–23), the return of Elijah (see Mk 9:11–13), and references to the Mosaic Law in Matthew's Sermon on the Mount. Luke omits exclusively Jewish titles, using "master" (teacher) for rabbi, "lawyer" for scribe, and "savior" for Messiah. Luke further emphasizes that Jesus is the *only* Lord. He wants to distinguish the unique Savior from gentile emperors who also called themselves lords.

Because it incorporates about 65 percent of Mark's gospel, Luke had to be written after Mark. Two passages in Luke (19:43–44 and 21:20) also imply that the author was aware of Jerusalem's destruction. Thus, scholars date Luke anywhere from 75 to 90. Both the gospel of Luke and the Acts of the Apostles were most likely composed sometime in the 80s.

### Who Was Luke?

**Three New Testament epistles mention Luke by name. Please read the references to discover the answers to the questions: Col 4:14, Phlm 1:24, 2 Tm 4:11.**

1. **What was Luke's profession?**
2. **Describe Luke's relationship with Paul.**

*Why? What? How?* Luke's prologue provides solid information on why Luke wrote his gospel, what it's about, and how he wrote it.

> Seeing that many others have undertaken to draw up accounts of the events that have reached their fulfillment among us, as these were handed down to us by those who from the outset were eyewitnesses and ministers of the word, I in my turn, after carefully going over the whole story from the beginning, have decided to write an ordered account for you, Theophilus, so that your Excellency may learn how well founded the teaching is that you have received (Lk 1:1–4).

Luke shows a concern with historical detail and literary purpose. As we shall see below, his interest in history helps him construct a unified work with Jerusalem as a central symbol in his presentation.

Luke dedicates his gospel to a certain *Theophilus*, a Greek name that means "lover of God." Whether Theophilus was an actual person or a symbol for all Christians, this name unites Luke's two-volume work. At the beginning of Acts, Luke writes:

> In my earlier work, Theophilus, I dealt with everything Jesus had done and taught from the beginning until the day he gave his instructions to the apostles he had chosen through the Holy Spirit, and was taken up to heaven (Acts 1:1–2).

If we look on Luke-Acts as a unit, we can detect Luke's master plan. It revolves around his belief in three periods of salvation history:

1) In the first two chapters of his gospel, Luke shows the relationship between Jesus and the history of Israel;

2) In the rest of the gospel, Luke gives an orderly account of the life, death, and resurrection of the Savior, showing how Jesus, Israel's promised Savior, has come for all people everywhere;

3) In Acts, Luke traces the rapid spread of the apostolic church through the Gentile world.

In his address to Theophilus, Luke states his major reason for writing. He wants to show Theophilus and all Christian readers that their instruction in the Christian faith is sound. *His purpose for writing the gospel was to strengthen their faith.* Second-century Gentile Christians lived in a world that both questioned and opposed Christianity. Luke-Acts is a masterful restatement and defense of Jesus' good news. It is also a faith-filled testimony about the continuing activity of the resurrected Lord and the Holy Spirit in history.

*Outline of Luke.* Luke is called the "historian of the church." This is an accurate portrayal of the evangelist who consciously links salvation history and ordinary history. For example, he situates the ministry of John the Baptist in both Roman and Jewish history by naming seven historical leaders:

> In the fifteenth year of Tiberius Caesar's reign, when Pontius Pilate was governor of Judea, Herod tetrarch of Galilee, his brother Philip tetrarch of the territories of Ituraea and Trachonitis, Lysanias tetrarch of Abilene, and while the high-priesthood was held by Annas and Caiaphas, the word of God came to John the son of Zechariah, in the desert (Lk 3:1–2).

Luke's gospel centers on Jerusalem. The gospel begins in Jerusalem with Zechariah and the birth of John the Baptist, as well as with Simeon and Anna prophesying in the Temple that Jesus is the promised Savior. As a youth of twelve, he astounds the teachers in Jerusalem and informs Mary and Joseph that he is about his Father's work in the holy city.

Although the first part of Jesus' public ministry takes place in Galilee, Luke continuously reminds us of the importance of Jerusalem. Pharisees and teachers come from there to criticize Jesus' teaching and crowds of Jerusalem's citizens seek him out to hear his teaching.

In Luke 9:51, Jesus "resolutely turned his face toward Jerusalem." This marks the beginning of the heart of Luke's gospel, the long journey from Galilee to Jerusalem. Along the way, Jesus tells his disciples: "Look, we are going up to Jerusalem, and everything that is written by the prophets about the Son of man is to come true" (Lk 18:31). With heart and mind set on his destiny in Jerusalem, Jesus journeys there to accomplish his Father's will. The gospel ends with Jesus telling his apostles to preach the forgiveness of sin to all nations, "beginning from Jerusalem." But he instructs them to await the descent of the Holy Spirit. Obeying Jesus, they remain in Jerusalem "full of joy; and they were continually in the Temple praising God" (Lk 24:53).

Below is a commonly accepted outline of Luke's gospel.

Prologue: 1:1–4

I. From the Jerusalem Temple to the End of the Galilean Ministry (1:5—9:50)

A. infancy narratives (1:5—2:52)
B. preparation for ministry (3:1—4:13)
C. Galilean ministry (4:14—9:50)

II. Journey from Galilee to Jerusalem (9:51—19:27)

III. Events in Jerusalem (19:28—24:53)
A. Jerusalem ministry (19:28—21:38)
B. the passion and death of Jesus (22—23)
C. the resurrection (24)

### Reading Luke

In this exercise, you will focus on a key theme of Luke's gospel, *Jesus as the universal savior*. Jesus' message of salvation is for everyone: Gentiles, outcasts, sinners.

Divide into five groups, each one taking a section of Luke's gospel. Note, discuss, and then report on examples of Jesus' universal message of love. Notice, in particular, what he says and does in relationship to the following people: the poor, Gentiles, women, Samaritans, sinners, and outcasts.

*The Readings...*

*Group 1:* 4:14—6:49
*Group 2*: 7:1—9:50
*Group 3*: 9:51—12:59
*Group 4*: 13:1—16:31
*Group 5*: 17:1—19:27

## Themes in the Gospel of Luke

***The spirit of the Lord is on me,***
***for he has anointed me***
***to bring the good news to the afflicted.***
***He has sent me to proclaim liberty to captives,***
***sight to the blind,***
***to let the oppressed go free,***
***to proclaim a year of favor from the Lord* (Lk 4:18–19).**

*Jesus Begins His Ministry (Lk 4:14–44).* Luke tells us that Jesus selected a passage from the prophet Isaiah (Is 61:1–2) to read at a synagogue service in his hometown of Nazareth.

> The spirit of Lord Yahweh is on me
> for Yahweh has anointed me.
> He has sent me to bring the news to the afflicted,
> to soothe the broken-hearted,
> to proclaim liberty to captives,
> release to those in prison,
> to proclaim a year of favor from Yahweh
> and a day of vengeance for our God.

In telling this story, Luke emphasizes the drama of the moment. He tells us that Jesus returned to Nazareth "in the power of the Spirit" very shortly after his temptations in the desert. At first, Jesus' townsfolk look at him with admiration. But then Jesus reveals the meaning of the text. In him, the prophecy about the Messiah is taking place. God's reign is present. What Isaiah has prophesied is happening right now. Through this scripture passage, Jesus shows the main outline of his ministry: he came to preach the gospel, to help people live freely, to perform acts of mercy, to work for justice, and to celebrate God's presence in the world.

Jesus' explanation astonishes his fellow citizens. When his indirect claim to be the promised Messiah sinks in, they become outraged. "Who is Jesus? Isn't he the son of Joseph? How could our carpenter neighbor be the promised one? It doesn't make sense."

Luke tells us that Jesus defends himself by saying no prophet ever receives honor in his own hometown. He points to the examples of Elijah and Elisha, who were also rejected by their contemporaries. As a result, Elijah and Elisha helped Gentiles. Jesus' reference to these two famous Hebrew prophets implies that the Messiah would also preach a *universal* message, one meant also for the Gentiles. This suggestion and Jesus' criticism enrages the people. They lead him to the brow of a hill in Nazareth, fully intending to throw him off, but Jesus escapes.

These verses in Luke's gospel are important for many reasons. First, they reveal what Jesus thought of his identity and how he conceived his mission. He is the Messiah, the Savior who has come to proclaim the gospel and put it into action. His mission is especially to the afflicted and oppressed, a major theme of Luke's gospel. Second, this scene at Nazareth foreshadows Jesus' public life. He meets with initial acceptance but later people reject him and put him to death. Third, the synagogue scene underscores two key themes in Luke's gospel: the Holy Spirit and the importance of prayer.

## ▪ journal ▪

**Describe a time when others rejected you. How did you cope with it?**

## ▪ discuss ▪

1. Give examples of this saying: "No prophet is ever accepted in his own country."
2. Review the five goals of Jesus' mission. Discuss practical ways today's youth can help the Lord accomplish each of them.

— preaching the gospel
— helping people to live freely
— doing acts of mercy
— working for justice
— celebrating God's presence in our midst

*The Role of the Holy Spirit.* The gospel of Luke and Acts highlight the role of the Holy Spirit in salvation history. Luke portrays salvation history as a dramatic unfolding of God's plan.

*Stage 1: Age of Promise.* Jesus announces that "today" God's covenant promises are being fulfilled. The Holy Spirit has singled him out to accomplish the Father's plan.

*Stage 2: The Time of Jesus.* Luke underscores that Jesus is the center of history. Guided by the Spirit, Jesus teaches a message of salvation for all. His miracles prove the power of his message, and the paschal mystery accomplishes our salvation.

*Stage 3: The Age of the Church.* The Holy Spirit empowers the early Christians to continue the gospel mission until Jesus comes in glory.

The Spirit appears frequently in Luke-Acts. For example, Mary becomes the mother of God through the power of the Holy Spirit (Lk 1:35). The Spirit moves the prophet Simeon to recognize the infant Jesus as the promised one (2:27). The Spirit descends on Jesus in the form of a dove (3:22). Jesus is led into the desert by the Spirit (4:1) and emerges (4:14) to begin his public ministry preaching with power. He prays full of power in the Spirit (10:21) and teaches us how to pray for the Holy Spirit (11:13).

You will notice in these citations how much the Holy Spirit leads and directs Jesus in his own ministry. Luke repeatedly says the Holy Spirit gives courage to the disciples to proclaim the message. The Spirit's presence impels the early Christians to preach the gospel throughout the Roman Empire, opening hearts and enabling the word to fall on fertile ground.

Jesus' public ministry begins with the Spirit leading Jesus in his work of salvation; Acts ends with St. Paul quoting another passage from Isaiah, and proclaiming that the Spirit will continue his work of conversion until the end of time: "You must realize, then, that this salvation of God has been sent to the gentiles; and they will listen to it" (Acts 28:28).

## The Spirit in Acts

Answer the following questions by checking the passages in Acts.

1. What does the Spirit enable one to do? (Acts 2:17–18)
2. What gesture is associated with giving the power of the Spirit? (Acts 8:17, 9:17)
3. What emotional state does the Spirit often bring? (Acts 13:51)

*The Power of Prayer in Jesus' Ministry.* Closeness to the Holy Spirit and the power of prayer went hand-in-hand in Jesus' ministry. The message we should learn is simple: followers of Jesus should pray often as Jesus did. Prayer is not mainly a task of "informing" God. Rather it helps "form" and "reform" us.

Jesus prays often in Luke's gospel. He prayed at his baptism (3:21). He often withdrew to lonely places such as the desert to pray (5:16). Before choosing his apostles, he prayed for a full night on a mountainside (6:12). Before Peter proclaimed him the Christ, Jesus prayed (9:18), meditating over the various beliefs people had about him. Jesus told Peter that he prayed for him in a special way. He prayed at his transfiguration. While hanging on the cross, Jesus utters the most moving prayer of all: "Father, forgive them; they do not know what they are doing" (23:34).

Jesus also teaches others to pray. He gives the disciples the Lord's Prayer, which we also call the Our Father. He encourages his followers to pray always (21:36) and to pray in a special way for the Holy Spirit (11:13). Jesus tells them not to lose heart when they pray, to persist in prayer, trusting that God will give them what is good for them (11:9–13).

Jesus' example shows us the perfect way to pray — seeking God's will in all we do. Picture Jesus in the Garden of Gethsemane. He knows that if he does not flee his enemies will arrest and crucify him. He fears death. But he loves his Father even more: "Father,. . .if you are willing, take this cup away from me. Nevertheless, let your will be done, not mine" (22:42). Every time we recite the Lord's Prayer sincerely, we share in Jesus' prayer: "Your will be done!"

Luke tells us that prayer is essential for the Christian life. We must take time to be alone, to put ourselves in the presence of God, and to ask for the strength of the Holy Spirit. If we do, God will draw us close to his Son and bring us what we need to live the gospel with joy and conviction.

■ *journal* ■

**Please read Lk 18:1–8. Write your own interpretation of this parable.**

## Self-Evaluation on Prayer

____ 1. When I pray: a.) I am very persistent; b.) I am persistent; c.) I give up easily.

____ 2. Jesus tells us to pray with forgiveness. a.) I forgive easily and forget; b.) I act hurt, but eventually forgive; c.) I hold grudges; d.) I get even when someone has harmed me.

____ 3. My prayers: a.) ask for what I need; b.) ask for what I want.

____ 4. The Our Father tells us to praise God ("hallowed be thy name"). I praise God in prayer: a.) often; b.) sometimes; c.) never.

____ 5. I believe God will answer my prayers. a.) yes; b.) no; c.) uncertain.

6. My prayer life:

When do I usually pray?

______________________________

Where do I usually pray?

______________________________

How often do I pray?

______________________________

7. When has prayer helped me?

______________________________

8. How do I define prayer?

______________________________

■ *discuss* ■

**Can you be a follower of Jesus and *not* pray? Explain.**

# The Parables of Jesus

In the last chapter, we studied some of the parables of God's reign. In this chapter, we will focus on parables that illustrate the joy of the gospel and Jesus as compassionate Messiah and universal Savior.

*Some Reflections on the Parables.* Recall that a parable is a vivid word picture that makes a single comparison between an event in daily life and a religious message. Jesus usually drew his images from common activities of his day: fishing, farming, weddings, baking bread, shepherding.

The parables contain the heart of Jesus' good news about the reign of God, repentance, and forgiveness. The parables ask us to reflect on our own lives in light of this good news.

The parables also give us a good idea of how Jesus handled himself with his opponents. Many of them served as a defense of his teaching. They proclaim God's goodness to everyone and challenge those who resist this message to rethink their prejudices.

*How to Read the Parables.* With a little work, you can figure out the primary meaning of most parables on your own. Consulting commentaries will enrich your understanding of a parable's message. Here are several rules to keep in mind as you interpret the parables.

Rule 1: Check the setting of the parable. To whom does Jesus address the parable? What has led up to it? Does Jesus tell it to defend his teaching or actions? Did the evangelist insert it here because he was developing a certain theme?

Rule 2: Understand what the story is saying as a story. Don't try to interpret the parable until you know what the story is about.

Rule 3: Find the main point of the story. It is usually at the end. Find a point of comparison to some theme in Jesus' teaching. Is Jesus talking about God, salvation, himself, forgiveness?

Rule 4: Try to state the theme in one sentence. Use this formula: "Just as... so ...." For example, for the parable of the sower: "Just as seed sown in good soil will increase, so God's reign will increase beyond human imagination despite the opposition it will meet."

## Parables and Themes

Below you will find a list of some key parables of Jesus organized according to their major themes. Read the parable in bold letters and write an interpretation of it in the space provided.

| Theme | Some Parables | Interpretation |
|---|---|---|
| 1. God's reign has begun and salvation is taking place. | Mustard Seed (Mk 4:30–32)<br>**Yeast (Lk 13:20–21)** | |
| 2. God's reign is a free gift. He calls everyone to enter. | Workers in the Vineyard (Mt 20:1–16)<br>**Wedding Banquet (Lk 14:16–24)** | |
| 3. God loves sinners. We should imitate God's love by forgiving others. | Unforgiving Servant (Mt 18:23–35)<br>**Lost Sheep and Lost Coin (Lk 15:3–10)** | |
| 4. The good news demands an immediate response. We must always be ready to act on it. | Hidden Treasure (Mt 13:44–46)<br>**Vigilant and Faithful Servants (Lk 12:35–48)** | |
| 5. God's reign requires repentance. (Ask for forgiveness, pray always, choose God above everything, be faithful, love everyone.) | The Wedding Feast (Mt 22:1–14)<br>Pharisee and Tax Collector (Lk 18:9–14)<br>**The Rich Fool (Lk 12:13–21)** | |
| 6. God's reign has a price. It may bring suffering, but we will gain our reward. | Last Judgment (Mt 25:31–46)<br>**Places at Table (Lk 14:7–14)** | |

## ▪ journal ▪

1. Read the following parables: children in the marketplace (Lk 7:31–35) and the friend at midnight (Lk 11:5–8).
2. Answer these questions about each.
   a. Who is the audience?
   b. Why did Jesus tell the parable?
   c. What does it mean?
   d. Which theme from the list above does it exemplify?
3. Rewrite each of these parables in a modern setting. Share what you have written.

*Joy and Peace (Lk 15:11–32).* Luke's gospel radiates the joy and peace of Jesus. These themes are evident from the opening verses of the gospel. For example, the angel's announcement to Mary that she is to be the mother of God results in Mary's beautiful hymn of joy, the Magnificat. The birth of the Messiah brings joy in heaven as the angels glorify God and announce peace. Frightened shepherds experience the joy and peace of Jesus as they come in from the fields to worship him.

During Jesus' public life, the crowds rejoice over Jesus' mighty works. His closest companions also experience joy working for him. For example, the seventy-two disciples Jesus sent out to preach returned from their journey rejoicing. When Jesus rides into Jerusalem during Holy Week, the crowds joyfully proclaim:

> *Blessed is he who is coming*
> as King *in the name of the Lord!*
> Peace in heaven
> and glory in the highest heavens! (Lk 19:38).

The most joyous occasion of all, though, is Jesus' resurrection. He greets his followers with peace and urges them to rejoice at what God has accomplished for them.

These twin themes of joy and peace come together in chapter 15 of Luke's gospel. It contains three important parables: the lost sheep, the lost coin, and the lost ("prodigal") son. Note the setting of these parables (15:1–2): The Pharisees and scribes had been criticizing Jesus for welcoming and eating with sinners. Jesus told these parables to defend his attitude and actions, showing them that he was simply imitating the love of his Father.

*The Parable of the Father's Love.* The parable of the prodigal son is misnamed. It's important to focus not on the wayward son, but on the boundless love of the father. Note how the younger son arrogantly asks for his inheritance ahead of time, then squanders it in reckless living. At the lowest point in his life, he realizes that he would be better off as his father's servant, so he returns home.

Fully expecting harsh judgment from his father, the youth is surprised when his father receives him back unconditionally. The son's return is an occasion of great rejoicing, a fact that disturbs his older brother. The father persists in his abundant love by assuring his older son: "All I have is yours" (15:31). Nevertheless, the return of the younger son is the source of the greatest rejoicing: "But it was only right we should celebrate and rejoice, because your brother here was dead and has come to life; he was lost and is found" (15:32).

*Jesus as Compassionate Messiah (Lk 7:36–50; 19:1–10).* For Luke, Jesus is a compassionate Messiah who has come to prove God's great love. For example, Jesus identifies with the poor and lowly. He himself comes to us humbly, being born in a manger. Shepherds, social outcasts, are the first to visit him. We know that his parents were also poor because Mary gave two turtledoves, the offering of the poor, at his presentation in the Temple.

Describing his own work to the disciples of John the Baptist, Jesus said he came to proclaim the gospel to the poor (7:22). Luke's gospel, more pointedly than any other, reassures the poor and warns the rich. For example, compare Luke's first beatitude to Matthew's:

| How blessed are you who are poor: the kingdom of God is yours (Lk 6:20). | How blessed are the poor in spirit: the kingdom of Heaven is theirs (Mt 5:3). |
|---|---|

Luke adds to this blessing a warning to the rich:

> But alas for you who are rich: you are having your consolation now.
> Alas for you who have plenty to eat now: you shall go hungry.
> Alas for you who are laughing now: you shall mourn and weep (6:24–25).

*Lazarus and the Rich Man.* Of all the evangelists, only Luke tells us the story of Lazarus and the rich man. The poor man, Lazarus, suffered throughout his life, longing for the scraps that fell from the rich man's table. But the rich man did not respond to the suffering Lazarus. When Lazarus died, he received his eternal reward; when the rich man died, he received eternal suffering in hell. Through this parable Jesus warns that those who have plenty in this life must share with those who have less. Generosity and compassion for the poor and outcast are mandatory for the followers of Jesus.

One rich man who heard Jesus' call was the tax collector Zacchaeus, who scrambled up a tree to catch a glimpse of Jesus. When Jesus saw Zacchaeus, he asked to stay with him. Zacchaeus, filled with joy, received Jesus into his home and into his heart. Many people complained about Jesus staying with Zacchaeus, whom they considered a sinner. By reaching out to Zacchaeus, Jesus was enacting a living parable of God's love for the sinner. Jesus' compassion moved this person to action: Zacchaeus promised that he would right his wrongs and give half of his wealth to the poor.

*Jesus as Universal Savior (Lk 10:25–37 and 15:8–10).* Luke's compassionate messiah is also the savior of all people. Consider the message in the parable of the good Samaritan. Jesus tells the story of the compassionate Samaritan to demonstrate that everyone is our neighbor. Because Jews and Samaritans had been bitter enemies for many generations, Jesus shocks his listeners with the truth that our neighbors include even our enemies.

Through this story, Jesus taught the same lesson he taught in the Sermon on the Mount: "I say this to you, love your enemies" (Mt 5:44) and "So always treat others as you would like them to treat you" (Mt 7:12). He also taught that we should break through our prejudices and imitate our loving God by embracing everyone — even our enemies.

*The Gospel of Women.* Luke's gospel is often called "the gospel of women." Mary, Jesus' mother, is the perfect model of faith. Elizabeth and Anna proclaim Jesus' true identity from the very beginning of his life. Women follow Jesus as disciples and remain faithful to him to his death. Mary Magdalene is the first to announce his resurrection.

Jesus also includes women as the key figures in several of his parables. In fact, in the parable of the lost coin, Jesus compares a woman's rejoicing when she finds a coin to God's rejoicing over a repentant sinner.

Jesus' attitude toward women seems to have been in marked contrast to the attitudes of many rabbis and others of his time. He treated women as equals in the reign of God, faithful disciples who heard the word of God and acted on it.

*Conclusion.* Luke's gospel is a wonderful summary of the good news of Jesus. In it we find the proclamation of God's universal salvation in Jesus Christ. Jesus associates with all kinds of people: the humble, the poor, the despised, outcasts, and sinners. The good news is that no one is excluded from God's love. But Luke also reminds us that the followers of Jesus must imitate him. We do this by praying, allowing the Spirit to live in us, and loving as he loved. Our love must extend in a special way to the hurting and needy.

---

## Real Life

Suppose someone came up to you on the street and asked for a handout. What would you do? (Check off any real possibilities for you.)

____ a. Pretend you didn't hear the person.

____ b. Give some money simply to get rid of the person.

____ c. Tell the person to leave you alone.

____ d. Give directions to the local church or another social agency.

____ e. Offer to buy the person what he or she needed, for example, groceries.

____ f. Walk quickly away.

____ g. Judge the person's appearance and respond accordingly.

____ h. Other: ________________________________

**discuss**

**Share stories of something like this that happened to you. Discuss what you did. Then discuss how we, as Christians, should respond to situations like this.**

**journal**

The dictionary defines *joy* as "a condition or feeling of great pleasure or happiness; delight." Reflect on the following questions in your journal.

1. What were the three most joyful occasions of your life? Briefly describe them.
2. Why did you delight in these events? Ask yourself questions such as: Were other people involved? Who were they? How did I feel about myself? Was I active or passive? How much did my own attitude give rise to my happiness?

---

## ▪ focus questions ▪

1. Identify the author of Luke's gospel. What is unique about this author among the four evangelists?
2. Give a probable date and place for the composition of Luke.
3. Discuss three examples from Luke's gospel that show his concern about stressing the universality of Jesus' message.
4. Why did Luke write his gospel? Identify Theophilus, the person to whom he addressed it.
5. Explain how Jerusalem plays a central role in the organization of Luke-Acts.
6. Jesus' quotation of a prophecy of Isaiah in a synagogue in Nazareth outlined the agenda for his public ministry. What were the five elements in this ministry?
7. Discuss several incidents in Luke in which the Holy Spirit plays a prominent role.
8. According to Luke, what are the three stages of salvation history?
9. Why and for what should Christians pray?
10. What is a parable?
11. How should we interpret parables? Discuss the meaning of these parables: good Samaritan, prodigal son, Lazarus and the rich man.
12. Why are the parables of Jesus so important?
13. Discuss at least four themes in the parables of Jesus and list a parable that illustrates each theme.
14. Explain why the gospel should make us joyful. Illustrate your points with examples from Luke's gospel.
15. Discuss examples to show that Luke's gospel stresses a compassionate Jesus who loves everyone.
16. Who in today's world might be like Zacchaeus?
17. Why is Luke's gospel sometimes called "the gospel of women"?

## ▪ vocabulary ▪

**Copy the meaning of these words into your journal.**

citation
consumerism
impel
vigilant

### ■ *exercise* ■

Write your own version of the parable of the good Samaritan. Substitute modern elements in the story. Share this with the class.

---

## Prayer Reflection

Recall the steps for a biblical meditation: Assume a comfortable position. Relax. Recall the presence of the Lord. Feel his love engulf you.

Now turn to Luke 7:36–50. Imagine that you are a guest at Simon's house. Engage all your senses. What do you see, hear, feel, smell? What is Simon serving for dinner? Turn your attention to Jesus. What is he saying? What does he look like?

Now see the woman run in from off the street and the commotion she causes. What is she doing? What do you feel about this? How are the other dinner guests reacting to this scene? Listen carefully to what Jesus says to Simon.

Finally, savor Jesus' gentleness to the woman. Hear his reassuring words and feel their impact on you:

> "For this reason I tell you that her sins, many as they are, have been forgiven her, because she has shown such great love.... Your faith has saved you; go in peace" (Lk 8:47, 50).

### ■ *reflection* ■

Where does sin have control in your life? Do you believe Jesus can forgive your sins? Are you willing to take them to him and hear his message of love, forgiveness, and peace?

### ■ *resolution* ■

Examine your conscience this week on those actions and attitudes that keep you from being a more loving person. Resolve to celebrate the sacrament of reconciliation at the earliest possible time.

---

*chapter 7*

# The Gospel of John
## Sign and Glory

For this is how God loved the world:
he gave his only Son,
so that everyone who believes in him may not perish
but may have eternal life.

— John 3:16

**In This Chapter**

**We will explore:**

- **authorship, date, audience, and outline of John**
- **the prologue (Jn 1:1–18)**
- **book of signs**
- **book of glory**
- **the resurrection of Jesus**

Martin Luther, the great Protestant reformer, called John 3:16 "the heart of the Bible, the Gospel in miniature." Even a child can understand its simple message. Throughout John's gospel, we find simple but profound images such as life and death, light and darkness, flesh and spirit, glory and eternal life. These images help us explore the meaning of Jesus and the salvation he has won for us.

In contrast to this simplicity, John's gospel is also characterized by long, well-developed theological discourses. In these, Jesus reveals the Father and teaches deep truths about himself and important aspects of Christian life. John's discourses have a recognizable pattern: an *event* triggers a *dialogue* between Jesus and others. This, in turn, results in a *monologue* in which Jesus gives a theological reflection.

John's gospel also includes many important scenes that do not appear in the synoptics. For example, John mentions Jesus' attendance at three Passover celebrations in Jerusalem. This helps us calculate Jesus' public ministry as lasting two to three years. Other unique features in John are the following gospel scenes: the wedding at Cana, the encounter with Nicodemus, the dialogue at the well with the Samaritan woman, the healing at the pool of Bethesda, the raising of Lazarus, and the washing of the apostles' feet at the Last Supper.

Finally, John allows Jesus' divine nature to shine through. His portrait of Jesus shows a man self-confident in the face of death. The author of John projected his resurrection faith back into the life of Christ. There is no doubt in John's gospel about who Jesus is or why he came. Jesus is the majestic Son of God who reveals the Father.

## Washing Feet

Please read John 13:1–20, the scene of Jesus washing the feet of the apostles at the Last Supper. This parable-in-action challenges all of us to imitate the Lord, to serve others as he served us.

What is your "service quotient"? How well do you respond to others? How important has service to others been in the past? Rate yourself using the following scale:

5 — excellent performance
4 — very good
3 — good
2 — fair
1 — poor

____ 1. At home, I discuss issues of social concern. For example, I have begun family discussions on prejudice, economic justice, consumerism, war and peace issues, etc.

____ 2. I have tried to befriend classmates who are lonely or rejected.

____ 3. Right now I am participating in a school or parish program of service to others.

____ 4. I give some of my allowance or earnings to people in need, for example, to the missions or to a homeless shelter.

____ 5. I have spoken up to defend people or minority groups who have been ridiculed.

____ 6. Within the past three months, I have helped someone without expecting any pay (for example, yard work or shoveling for old folks in the neighborhood, visiting or helping a sick or handicapped person, babysitting).

____ 7. I read the daily newspaper or a weekly news magazine and regularly try to follow some of the major social issues of our day.

____ 8. I have considered and even read about or discussed a future service-oriented career.

____ 9. In the past three months, I have personally testified to my faith.

*Interpretation*: Add your score and divide by 9 to see how well you are doing.

■ *discuss* ■

1. Can you call yourself a Christian and not serve others? Explain.
2. "Service is fine, but I have to get an education first. I'll become involved once I have a career."
3. List and discuss three practical ways teens can serve the local community.

■ *journal* ■

**In a short reflective essay, discuss what you would really like to do for a career. List several ways your choice could be a way to "wash others' feet."**

## Authorship, Date, Audience, and Outline of John

*Who? Where?* St. Irenaeus, writing around the year 180, attributed the fourth gospel to John, the "beloved disciple." Irenaeus claimed that this John, son of Zebedee and brother of James, wrote toward the end of his life at Ephesus in Asia Minor. For centuries this was the most popular tradition about the authorship of the fourth gospel.

Today, however, scholars believe Irenaeus may have confused John the apostle with another John, a church elder and disciple of the apostle. Students of the fourth gospel note its complex nature and suggest that it was written in several stages and edited by different people. For example, we can see that some material appears twice with only slight changes in the wording (compare 6:35–50 and 6:51–58). Chapter 21 also appears to be an appendix that someone other than the original evangelist tacked on to the end of the gospel.

The most common theory today among Catholic scholars is that the apostle John's experience with Jesus is the foundation of the gospel. A solid tradition places him in Ephesus (in present-day Turkey) where he likely gathered around him a community of believers. These disciples took the apostle's testimony, meditated on his words, and later produced a gospel that addressed the concerns of their own Christian community. Thus John, the beloved disciple of Jesus, is the authority behind the gospel: "This disciple is the one who vouches for these things and has written them down, and we know that his testimony is true" (Jn 21:24).

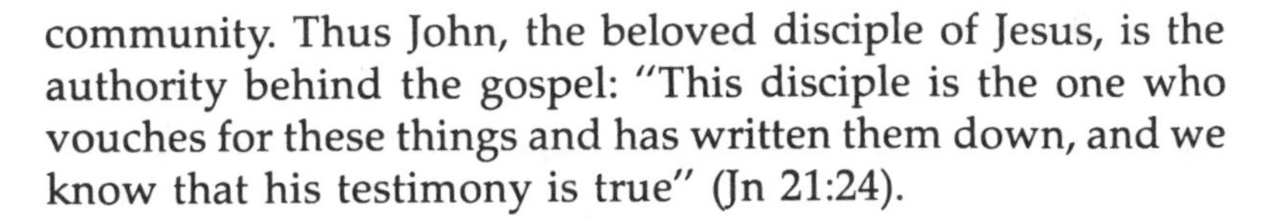

### discuss

Read the following passages about John, Zebedee's son, and discuss the following questions.

| | |
|---|---|
| Jn 13:23 | Jn 20:2–10 |
| Jn 19:26 | Jn 21:7, 20–23 |

1. How did Jesus specially favor this disciple?
2. Describe him in relation to Peter. What does his stepping aside to allow Peter to enter the tomb first signify (20:3–5)?

*When?* The most popular opinion for the date of the writing of John's gospel is sometime between 90 and 100. A short fragment from John's gospel is the earliest fragment of any New Testament book in existence. Found in Egypt, this fragment, known as the John Rylands fragment, is written in Greek on papyrus and dates from around 130. It proves that the fourth gospel must have had wide circulation throughout the Mediterranean basin only thirty or forty years after its composition.

*What? Why?* Although the author of John's gospel probably knew of one or more of the synoptic gospels, he does not rely heavily on any of them, preferring to use as sources independent traditions preserved in the churches influenced by the disciples of John.

The gospel was written for a somewhat diverse audience. Among John's readers were Jewish-Christians who suffered at the hands of other Jews. You may recall that Christians were expelled from the synagogues after the revolt against Rome. John's community probably left Palestine and emigrated to Ephesus.

The gospel also suggests that many Samaritan converts were part of John's community (see Jn 4:4–42). And, if the gospel were composed in a city in Asia Minor, undoubtedly many Gentile Christians would also have been part of the fourth gospel's audience.

Commentators offer various reasons as to why John wrote his gospel. For example, he may have been trying to correct heretical ideas that denied Jesus' divinity. Other scholars feel the gospel may have contradicted disciples of John the Baptist who still believed that he was the Messiah. The fourth gospel emphasizes that John the Baptist is subordinate to Jesus.

The gospel itself clearly states the reason for its existence:

> There were many other signs that Jesus worked in the sight of the disciples, but they are not recorded in this book. These are recorded so that you may believe that Jesus is the Christ, the Son of God, and that believing this you may have life through his name (Jn 20:30–31).

John's purpose is to strengthen Christian belief in Jesus as God's Son and win over new converts. John does not try to recall all the details of Jesus' public ministry; the synoptics fill in this picture. John zeroes in on Jesus' identity as the revealer of God, unique Son of the Father, and Savior of the world. His emphasis is on theology rather than on storytelling (Mark), teaching (Matthew), or history (Luke).

The theme of eternal life is central to John's gospel. Because Jesus is God, he lives forever. He is eternal life. Through faith in Jesus, the Lord offers us eternal life right now. Jesus invites us to begin a personal, eternal relationship with him even during our earthly life "so that our joy may be complete" (1 Jn 1:4).

*How?* John drew on sources similar to those found in the synoptic gospels. He had two major sources. The first was a collection of miracles, called a "signs source." The synoptics contain some of the seven signs John records, but unique to John are the changing of water into wine at Cana and the raising of Lazarus. The discourses connected with these miracles were probably arranged, developed, and preached in the circle of John the apostle's own followers. The second major source was a version of the passion and resurrection stories. This would have been in circulation for years before any of the gospels were written.

John weaves into the fabric of his gospel several key themes that appear throughout the work. One of these, the theme of eternal life, we referred to above. Here are some others to keep in mind as you read John.

| THEME | EXPLANATION | APPLICATION |
|---|---|---|
| Jesus Christ, Son of God | Jesus is God's unique Son, both fully God and fully human. As God's Son, only he can reveal the Father fully. | Jesus is trustworthy. Listening to Jesus puts us on the path to truth and life. |
| Believe | Look to the signs Jesus performs and believe. Belief leads to eternal life. | Response to Jesus means believing in him — his life, words, death, and resurrection. |
| Holy Spirit | Jesus promised a Paraclete who would guide, comfort, and counsel Christians. Through the Spirit, the Lord will be present in believers. | The Spirit enables us to believe and understand Jesus' teaching. Allowing the Spirit to live within us helps us experience the love of the risen Lord. |
| Resurrection | Jesus lives! On the third day, he rose from the dead, a fact testified to by the apostles and others. It is the basic fact of Christian faith. | Believe in Jesus! He is the resurrection and the life. If we die united to him, we will also live forever. |

*Outline of John's Gospel.* Even though John is a rich, complex, theologically profound gospel, its outline is simple: a short, but extremely important prologue, followed by two major sections — the book of signs, which treats Jesus' public ministry, and the book of glory, which begins with the Last Supper and continues through Easter Sunday — and concluding with an epilogue, probably added later, which records the resurrection appearances in Galilee.

Prologue: "Word made flesh" . . . . . . . . . . . . . . . . . . 1:1–18

Part 1: Book of Signs . . . . . . . . . . . . . . . . . . . . 1:19—12:50

A. Choosing Disciples (1:19—4:54)
B. Disputes ["Who is Jesus?"] (5:1—10:42)
C. The Raising of Lazarus and Aftermath (11:1—12:50)

Part 2: Book of Glory . . . . . . . . . . . . . . . . . . . . 13:1—20:31

A. The Last Supper (13:1—17:26)

B. The Passion (18:1—19:42)
C. The Resurrection (20:1–29)

Epilogue: Appearances in Galilee . . . . . . . . . . . . . . . . .21:1–25

## The Prologue (Jn 1:1–18)

The prologue was originally an early Christian hymn adopted by the evangelist to introduce his gospel. It contains many of the central theological themes of the gospel.

*Theme 1: Who Is Jesus?* Note the opening words of John's gospel:

> In the beginning was the Word:
> the Word was with God
> and the Word was God (Jn 1:1).

John unveils Jesus' true identity as the Word of God who has existed forever. This very Word of God is God himself.

By using the expression "Word of God," the evangelist was drawing on a concept that would appeal to both Jewish-Christian and Gentile-Christian readers. In the Hebrew scriptures, "the Word of God" (*logos* in Greek) referred to God's activity at the creation of the world. God creates through his Word. For example, when he speaks, creatures come into being. "The Word of God" also was a symbol for God's Wisdom. In salvation history, God's Wisdom is associated with creation, the Law, God's revelation through the prophets, and his close presence among his people.

"Word of God" also meant something to Gentiles immersed in Greek philosophy. For some Greek philosophers, the Logos was the spiritual principle that holds the world together. Others believed that only the Logos could reveal the knowledge that is the key to salvation.

These rich ideas — the creative Word, source of true wisdom and knowledge, God's presence among his people — blend wonderfully in John's prologue. Verse 14 is the climax:

> The Word became flesh,
> he lived among us
> [literally "he pitched his tent among us"],
> and we saw his glory,
> the glory that he has from the Father as only Son of the Father,
> full of grace and truth.

*Theme 2: The Incarnation.* Verse 1 identifies Jesus as God's pre-existing Word who is God; verse 14 tells us that God became human. This is the doctrine of the *Incarnation,* the mystery of God's only Son becoming truly human in Jesus. Jesus is God-in-the-flesh. In Jesus we can perceive God's *glory,* a Hebrew concept that refers to the visible revelation of the power of the invisible God. In and through Jesus, God's glory — his power, radiance, and love — shines forth. Verses 1 and 14 also introduce a special movement that we see in John's gospel: Christ comes to us from above (1:1–13); he reveals the Father to us and takes us to him (1:14–18).

*Theme 3: Testimony.* The prologue assigns to John the Baptist his proper role. He came to bear witness to the light that is Christ, testifying to his pre-existence. The Baptist prefigures all the others who will testify for Jesus later in the gospel: the Samaritan woman, Martha and the crowd at Lazarus' raising, the Twelve, and the "beloved disciple." Jesus himself, as well as the Father and the Spirit, provides testimony for his identity as God's only Son. Jesus' seven miracles also attest to his mission and identity.

*Theme 4: Major Contrasts.* Finally, the prologue introduces some of the major contrasts in the gospel. These include:

- the light of Christ versus the darkness of the world that refuses to acknowledge Jesus;
- unbelief versus life-giving faith in Jesus that makes us children of God;
- truth versus untruth.

## Book of Signs

The synoptic gospels understand miracles as demonstrations of the coming of God's reign. The concept of miracle in John's gospel takes a different turn than in the synoptics. John reports seven *signs* (*semeia* in Greek), marvelous events that *reveal* Jesus and his Father. John's gospel insists that we can only grasp the point of Jesus' signs if we have faith in him. Faith leads to understanding the deeper meaning of these seven signs. The author of John usually provides a long discourse after each miracle/sign to help the reader comprehend the significance of Jesus. These discourses constantly remind us that belief in Jesus helps us gain eternal life.

Let's turn to a brief explanation of each sign and a reflection on several of the discourses. Please read the passages noted.

*Sign One: Changing Water Into Wine at Cana (Jn 2:1–12).* Weddings are festive occasions, symbols of new life and loving union. This first sign shows that Jesus can bring us new life. He can change us into loving members of one body just as he changed ordinary water into the festive drink of fellowship. Water in this miracle can be seen as representing the old covenant, while wine represents the new covenant that brings us spiritual life through communion with Jesus.

*Key Discourse: Jesus and the Samaritan Woman (Jn 4:1–26).* Before moving on to Jesus' second sign, John reports two key discourses, one with Nicodemus, a Pharisee (3:1–21), a second with a Samaritan woman at Jacob's well. Jesus boldly ignored first-century Jewish social conventions by speaking in a public place to a Samaritan woman, known even among her fellow Samaritans as a sinner. Jesus' contemporaries would be scandalized by this behavior. What is the meaning of this meeting?

Jesus met the woman where she was and challenged her. He spoke of "living water," a new life that only he, the Messiah, could give. The woman wondered aloud how Jesus could provide this special water. Jesus patiently led her out of confusion. The woman was thirsting for knowledge and acceptance, and Jesus gave her what she needed. He revealed that he was the Messiah, the source of eternal life that can refresh and renew. He also told her that his life enables a person to worship God in spirit and truth.

### ▪ discuss ▪

1. What do you imagine the woman told her fellow Samaritans about Jesus? Would this have caused them to believe in him? Why or why not? (Give evidence for your response.)
2. Discuss several possible meanings for water as a basic human symbol and a Christian symbol. Explain several things Jesus could have meant by using this symbol.
3. How can you help lead others to Jesus, the living water?

### ▪ journal ▪

**What do you most thirst for in your life right now? How can Jesus help quench that thirst?**

*Sign Two: Cure of the Official's Son (Jn 4:46–54).* This second sign shows that the power of Jesus' word is enough to heal the son of a court official from the town of Capernaum. The father's faith prompted Jesus to act. This sign teaches that faith in Jesus can rescue us from spiritual death. It also teaches the power of intercessory prayer. The Lord will notice and respond to our concern for others as he did for the father who wanted health for his boy.

*Sign Three: Cure of the Paralytic at the Pool (Jn 5:1–47).* Jesus heals a man who was lame for thirty-eight years, and he associates this healing with forgiveness of sin. The healing takes place on the sabbath, which goes against the command to do no work on the sabbath. The discourse following this dramatic miracle underscores the issues at stake. Jesus claims to be equal to God. Like the Father, the Son gives life whenever he wants and to whomever he wants. Finally, the Father gives his Son the right to judge others according to their deeds. The point of this third sign is that Jesus is the source of life. We must believe in him to gain eternal life.

You may have noticed in this passage the evangelist's hostile use of the expression "the Jews." Several times in John's gospel the antagonism between Jesus and "the Jews" is so intense that it appears *anti-Semitic* (prejudiced against the Jews), even though Jesus and all of his early disciples were Jews. Scholars tell us that John uses this expression to refer to those people who refuse to accept Jesus because he seems to demand that they abandon their beliefs and practices. These Jews felt that accepting Jesus would lead to a loss of their identity.

**discuss**

1. **What is anti-Semitism? What are some examples of it?**
2. **"To be anti-Semitic is to be anti-Christian." Explain the truth of this proposition.**

*Signs Four and Five: Feeding the Five Thousand and Walking on Water (Jn 6:1–14; 16–21).* Jesus feeds the hungry crowd following him, but he has to escape their attempt to make him king. This took place close to the time of the Passover feast. John's long dialogue on the "Bread of Life" (6:25–70) explains the symbolism of this sign. Jesus has replaced the manna of the Exodus. He is the new bread God has given to them, their source of eternal life. Through him all will pass over from death to new life.

> "I am the bread of life.
> No one who comes to me will ever hunger;
> no one who believes in me will ever thirst" (6:34–35).

Jesus teaches that his followers need to eat his flesh and drink his blood, a clear reference to the eucharist. The eucharist brings about an intimate relationship between Jesus and his friends. He abides in us and we in him. As the Father is the source of Jesus' life, so Jesus is the source of our life.

This shocking teaching about his body and blood caused many to abandon Jesus. But Peter and the apostles put their trust in him: "Lord, to whom shall we go? You have the message of eternal life, and we believe; we have come to know that you are the Holy One of God" (6:68–69).

Jesus' walking on water revealed that he was indeed God's Holy One. God and Jesus are one. Despite the storms of life, the disciples of Jesus need never fear. Jesus, God himself, is with us and will never leave us.

## Reading Scripture

John 8:13–59 is a long dialogue between Jesus and his enemies. Jesus testifies on his own behalf. His self-defense culminates in verse 58. Please read this verse and answer the two questions below.

1. What is Jesus claiming?
2. What reaction does it bring about?

Then read John 18:1–11. Explain the meaning of verse 6. Why did the guards fall down?

*Sign Six: Cure of the Blind Man (Jn 9:1–41).* The blind man obeys Jesus, washes in the Pool of Siloam, and receives his sight. He gradually comes to believe not only in the miracle but in Jesus as God's Son. He refuses to criticize Jesus, even though it leads to his expulsion from the synagogue. This detail was important to John's audience because as followers of Jesus they had been expelled from the synagogues.

John returns to the symbolism of the prologue. Jesus is the light that has come into the world. His truth dispels the darkness of ignorance. His light gives us direction and overcomes the darkness of sin. He asks for faith in him to overcome spiritual blindness. Some Pharisees have been blind to Jesus' goodness. Their own prejudices about Sabbath observance made them unable to see God's presence in their midst. Jesus says spiritual blindness is worse than physical blindness (9:41).

*Sign Seven: Raising of Lazarus (Jn 11:1–44).* This most important sign prefigures Jesus' own death and resurrection. On his way to Jerusalem, Jesus learns of his friend's mortal illness, but he waits so his Father can glorify him through a marvelous sign.

To Lazarus' grieving sister Martha, Jesus proclaims that faith allows the believer to participate in his paschal mystery.

> "I am the resurrection.
> Anyone who believes in me, even though that person dies, will live,
> and whoever lives and believes in me
> will never die.
> Do you believe this?" (Jn 11:25–26).

Jesus weeps for his friend Lazarus. He also prays to his Father, thanking him for answering his prayer. Finally, he calls Lazarus out of the grave. The dead man comes out and is freed of his burial clothes, a sign of our being freed from death.

Lazarus' raising causes many to believe. However, some of Jesus' enemies decide to eliminate him because they fear his popularity among the people and possible Roman reprisals. Caiaphas, the high priest, states that it is better for one man to die so that the nation will survive. John uses *irony* here in having Caiaphas unknowingly state the truth: Jesus' death has indeed saved all people.

This seventh miracle sums up all the other signs and pulls together many of John's major theological themes: Jesus is the way to life; he is the resurrection; he is God; we must have faith if we want to gain eternal life.

▪ *discuss* ▪

**What is ironical about the Samaritan woman's question about Jesus' greatness (Jn 4:12)?**

## Book of Glory

The second part of John's gospel — the Book of Glory — consists of two major sections: the Last Supper discourses (13:1—17:26) and Jesus' death and resurrection (18:1—20:31). In the Last Supper discourses, Jesus prepares his apostles for his hour of glory and instructs them on how to live after his resurrection. His passion, death, and resurrection reveal

God's love for us and mark Jesus' triumph and the victory of salvation he has won for us.

*The Last Supper Discourses.* Three words summarize the major themes of this section: service (Jn 13), love (Jn 14:1—16:4), and unity (Jn 17:1–26). John's gospel reports that the Last Supper occurred on the day on which the lambs were slaughtered for the Passover meal. The Jews sacrificed lambs to recall Yahweh releasing the Israelites from slavery in Egypt. Jesus is the Lamb of God whose sacrifice on the cross has freed all people from the slavery of sin. Every eucharist recalls and re-enacts in an unbloody manner Jesus' sacrifice for us.

Jesus began his celebration of the meal with a highly significant act. He, the Master, humbled himself by washing the feet of his disciples, a task even a slave was not required to perform. Peter objected to this act of humility, but Jesus performed it as an example. All his followers must imitate him. We must serve as he serves. Jesus wants us to attend to the needs of others. As one preacher put it, "The world cannot always understand one's profession of faith, but it can understand service."

Jesus reassures his disciples, telling them not to be troubled.

> "I am the Way; I am Truth and Life.
> No one can come to the Father except through me.
> If you know me, you will know my Father too.
> From this moment you know him and have seen him"
> (14:6–7).

Once again Jesus asks for belief in him, promising that if we ask for anything in his name he will do it. Our way to the Father is through him since Jesus and the Father are one.

Jesus also promises to send the Holy Spirit, the Paraclete — a counselor, helper, advocate. The Holy Spirit will open our minds and hearts, helping us understand and live Jesus' teaching.

Above all, Jesus teaches us to keep his commandments, especially his command to love. Love unites us to the Lord. Among its fruits are peace and joy.

Chapter 15 of John is one of the most important passages in the entire New Testament. In it, Jesus tells of his great love for us. As the Father loves him, so he loves us. He is the vine, we are the branches. We must remain attached to him. Loving as he loved is the principle of life that keeps Jesus' life in us. Reflect on these key passages:

> "No one can have greater love
> than to lay down his life for his friends.
> You are my friends,...
> You did not choose me,
> no, I chose you;...
> My command to you
> is to love one another" (15:13–14, 16–17).

This is the heart of the gospel. Jesus does not treat us like slaves. He has chosen us as his friends to continue his work of love. He dwells in us by the power of the Holy Spirit. This same Spirit protects us, guides us, enables us to love, and empowers us to witness to Jesus.

Jesus sees in each of us something so worthwhile that he wants us for his friends. He gives us life, cares for us, gives us many gifts, and brings us people who mean a lot to us. He loves us so much that he laid down his life for us. In return, he wants us to accept his love and friendship. He asks us to believe that we are lovable, and to ignore the world's false message of conditional love.

How do you show Jesus that you accept his gift of friendship? It's simple — love one another. The essence of the gospel message is to live a life of friendship with the Lord by loving one another.

The Last Supper ends with a passage known as the priestly prayer of Jesus. A priest is a mediator between God and people. In John 17, Jesus assumes a priestly role by interceding for us, by praying to his Father to watch over us so we can have a oneness in community with the Father, Son, and Spirit. He asks the Father to save us from the evil one and to make us cherish the truth.

This prayer reminds us that Jesus is active in today's world through us. The Lord's gentle touch is our touch. His forgiving words are heard on our lips. His compassionate concern for the lonely, the poor, the sick, the victims of injustice shows up in our kind deeds. His acceptance of others is seen in our eyes. As Jesus revealed the Father, our task is to reveal Jesus. This is an extraordinary privilege, but also a great responsibility.

## Growing in the Lord

Check how you are living Jesus' invitation at the Last Supper. Use the following rating system:

4 — excellent
3 — good
2 — fair
1 — poor

Friendship with the Lord:

____ spend time with him in prayer

____ see it as the most important relationship in my life

____ try to discover what he wants for me

____ consciously strive to imitate him

____ try to see him in other people

____ tell others about him

Love/service:

____ go out of my way to be helpful at home, school, work

____ seek out and respond to someone who needs me

____ often think of others' needs

____ practice self-denial

____ am dependable in my commitments

____ suffer inconvenience or ridicule for my Christian convictions

Unity:

____ repent when I sin (for example, celebrate the sacrament of reconciliation)

____ participate fully in Sunday Mass

____ receive holy communion regularly

____ try to make amends when I harm someone

### ▪ *discuss* ▪

What does it mean for today's teens to be friends of Jesus?

## The Resurrection of Jesus

Nothing exemplifies the glory of Jesus and his Father as much as the resurrection, the central event of our salvation. All four gospels report Jesus' resurrection, even though they do not agree on all the details or report the same appearances.

John's gospel tells us that Jesus appeared first to Mary Magdalene. At first she did not recognize him, mistaking him for the gardener, but when he called her by name, she knew it was the Lord. "Rabbuni, Master," she exclaimed. Jesus instructed her not to cling to him, because he had to ascend to his Father. Rather, she was to tell the disciples the joyous news of his triumph over death.

Imagine the apostles' shock and disbelief at Mary's report of Jesus' resurrection. However, ten of the apostles would soon know for themselves. They were afraid of their enemies and hiding behind a bolted door. Suddenly, Jesus appeared in their midst. He wished them peace and commissioned them to continue his work. He breathed on them, giving them the Holy Spirit, and instructed them to forgive sins in his name.

Eight days later, Jesus appeared to Thomas, who had not been with the apostles and doubted their report. When Thomas saw Jesus, he acknowledged Jesus' divinity, saying, "My Lord and my God." Jesus blesses all those who believe in him without seeing.

Originally, the gospel of John ended with Chapter 20. A later editor added Chapter 21, which reports Jesus' appearance to the apostles in Galilee. There Jesus helps the disciples catch fish and prepares a breakfast for them. This suggests his communion with them at eucharistic celebrations and his presence with them in their ministry of proclaiming the word to the ends of the earth. He also recommissions Peter, who three times had denied knowing Jesus, with a threefold promise of loving service.

---

### The Resurrection of Jesus

Read the resurrection narratives listed below. In your journal, answer the following questions about the similarities and differences.

| | |
|---|---|
| Mk 16:1–8; 9–20 | Mt 28:1–20 |
| Lk 24 | Jn 20 |

1. Does anyone witness the actual resurrection?
2. When does it take place?
3. What was the reaction of the women and the other disciples in all cases?
4. Where in Galilee did Jesus appear?
5. Where in Jerusalem did Jesus appear?

---

*Different Accounts.* Compare the various resurrection stories. They differ so much that it is impossible to blend them into one continuous narrative. Each evangelist chose from the available stories the ones that would be most helpful to his audience. We should not be surprised that the four gospels don't report the same stories. It's not unusual for eyewitnesses to give dissimilar accounts, especially if they've witnessed something shocking or amazing. In spite of the differences, however, all four gospels agree on the essentials:

■ *The tomb was empty.* This fact alone doesn't cause faith. For example, in John's gospel, Mary Magdalene was weeping because she thought someone stole Jesus' body. In Luke's account, the apostles think the women's report of the empty tomb is nonsense until they see for themselves, and even then they are amazed but do not necessarily believe in the resurrection.

The empty tomb is important because it corroborates that *something* happened. We are told that the enemies of the early Christians paid the guards to spread the rumor that Jesus' disciples carried away his body to prove their story, but they were never able to produce Jesus' corpse.

■ *Jesus appears to his disciples.* These appearances convinced a group of frightened men and women that the crucified Jesus was alive, that he was the Lord, God's Son. So life-changing were these appearances that, with the gift of the Holy Spirit, many early witnesses died proclaiming the truth of what they experienced.

Note several other aspects of Jesus' appearances. Jesus appeared to his disciples, who were sometimes slow to recognize him. They were not expecting the Lord to come back to life. They were discouraged and confused by his death.

They needed the Lord's own words of peace, instruction, and reassurance to help them come to belief in the resurrection.

The gospel accounts also insist that Jesus was not a ghost. Luke, for example, reports that the resurrected Jesus ate fish, while John's Jesus ate breakfast with his disciples. Furthermore, Jesus asks Thomas to touch his wounds. The resurrected Jesus is neither a ghost nor a dead person who has been revived as Lazarus was. He is alive in a transformed, glorified body that still has an aspect of "bodiliness" to it, including the wounds of his suffering.

Finally, read what St. Paul has to say about the resurrection (1 Cor 15:1–19). He tells us that Jesus made several appearances, including one to over five hundred people. At the time Paul was writing, in the early 50s, he assured his readers that many of these eyewitnesses were still alive. They could easily verify that the Lord rose from the dead and appeared to them.

■ *Jesus instructs his disciples and sends them the Holy Spirit to fulfill their mission.* Jesus helps his disciples reflect on scriptural prophecies concerning him (Lk 24:25–27). He commissions them to preach (Mt 28:18–20) and forgive sin (Jn 20:21–23). He tells them he will send them the Spirit who will empower them to accomplish marvels in his name (Lk 24:49).

■ *Meaning of the resurrection.* Jesus' resurrection is the most earth-shaking fact of salvation history. It proved Jesus' claims to be God's Son. Following the sacrifice on the cross, it accomplished our salvation. By conquering death, Jesus was victorious over sin and death, opening heaven's gates and winning our redemption.

As John's gospel repeatedly insists, Jesus brings us eternal life. Because the resurrection enables Jesus to live in us, we already share "eternal life," the life of the Lord who abides in us. Through the power of the Holy Spirit, Christians participate in the life, death, and resurrection of Jesus. The risen Lord promises that we will rise with him to eternal life in heaven.

The resurrection of Jesus gives new meaning to our lives. It says that death does not have the last word. Superabundant, eternal life with Jesus, in community with the Father and the Spirit and all others who love the Lord, is the central truth of our faith.

We should be joyful — our Lord lives and we will, too. We can find the resurrected Jesus in our Christian brothers and sisters. We can receive him in the eucharist where he comes to us under the forms of bread and wine. We can meet him in the lonely, the poor, the needy. We can find him in the depths of our spirits — comforting us, challenging us, assuring us of our worth, promising us his salvation.

John's gospel reminds us time and again: Believe! Believe and you will have life. A good question to end our study of John is simply, "Do you believe?"

## Do You Believe?

Check off those statements that you truly believe. Mark a **?** for any statement you are still questioning.

____ 1. Jesus is alive.

____ 2. Someday I will be with him for all eternity.

____ 3. I find the Lord in my Christian brothers and sisters.

____ 4. It is a privilege to receive and meet the risen Lord in the eucharist.

____ 5. I look forward to my own resurrection and the resurrection of all people.

____ 6. For me, life is filled with joy because death is not the end of everything!

### discuss

1. What might be the significance of Jesus appearing first to Mary Magdalene?
2. If the early Christians wished to fabricate the resurrection stories, would they have allowed the different stories of the resurrection appearances to remain inconsistent? Explain.
3. Are you convinced that Jesus lives? Why or why not?
4. Is the apostolic testimony about the resurrection of Jesus reliable? Explain.

## focus questions

1. Explain a couple of ways John's gospel differs from the synoptic gospels.
2. Who wrote the gospel of John? When and where was it probably composed? What was the evangelist's reason for composing it?
3. Discuss three major themes in John's gospel.
4. What does it mean to call Jesus the *Word of God*?
5. What is meant by the term "glory of God"?
6. What is the symbolic meaning of Jesus' first miracle at Cana?
7. How does John use the term *the Jews*? Why is anti-Semitism especially anti-Christian?
8. Why did so many of Jesus' followers abandon him after the sign of the bread?
9. Discuss the meaning of Jesus raising Lazarus from the dead.
10. Three words explain the themes of Jesus' Last Supper discourses: service, love, unity. Explain.
11. What is the symbolic meaning of Jesus' celebration of the Last Supper one day *before* the Passover feast?
12. What does it mean to be called Jesus' friends? According to John, what keeps us united to Jesus?
13. In what way did Jesus fulfill a priestly role in our salvation?
14. Describe the three resurrection appearances of Jesus in John's gospel. Why do the four gospels have different resurrection stories? Does this fact make them more or less believable? Explain.
15. On what essential points about the resurrection do all the gospels agree?
16. Discuss three important implications of the resurrection of Jesus. What does it mean?
17. Please identify the following terms:

    John Rylands fragment
    Incarnation
    Paraclete

## ▪ *journal* ▪

Read the following passages about light in John's gospel. Then answer these questions in your journal.

1. 3:19–21: How is sin related to darkness? What is the relationship between truth and light?
2. 8:12 and 11:9–10: What are at least two ways Jesus guides us in the light?
3. 12:35–36, 46: What makes us children of the light?
4. Why did Jesus choose the image of light? (Discuss several realities that light symbolizes and show how Jesus exemplifies them.)

## ▪ *vocabulary* ▪

**Copy the meaning of these words into your journal.**

**corroborate**
**epilogue**
**reprisal**

### Prayer Reflection

After putting yourself into a prayerful frame of mind, please turn to John 7:53—8:11, the touching scene of Jesus' forgiving the woman caught in adultery. (The earliest manuscripts of John do not include this story. It is written in the style of the synoptic gospels. Editors probably inserted it into the gospel at a later date.)

Picture yourself as the person caught in sin.

What sins do you need to overcome in your life? Ask Jesus to help you do this.

## ▪ *reflection* ▪

Who is it most difficult for you to forgive and why?

## ▪ *resolution* ▪

Think of a person you might be judging negatively. Resolve to forgive this person and accept him or her the way Jesus accepts the woman caught in adultery — and you.

*chapter* 8

# Acts of the Apostles

These remained faithful to the teaching of the apostles, to the brotherhood, to the breaking of bread and to the prayers.

And everyone was filled with awe; the apostles worked many signs and miracles.

And all who shared the faith owned everything in common; they sold their goods and possessions and distributed the proceeds among themselves according to what each one needed.

— Acts 2:42–45

**In This Chapter**

**We will look at:**

- **author, date, and similarities to Luke's gospel**
- **outline of Acts**
  - **— prologue (1:1–11)**
  - **— the church in Jerusalem (1:12—5:42)**
  - **— witness in Judea and Samaria (6:1—12:25)**
  - **— witness to the ends of the earth (13:1—28:31)**

Consider these examples of perseverance: The Greek philosopher Plato wrote the first sentence of his famous work the *Republic* nine different ways before he was satisfied with it. The poet John Milton got up at 4 a.m. everyday to have enough hours to complete his classic *Paradise Lost*. The painter Leonardo da Vinci worked on *The Last Supper* for ten years. He was often so lost in his work that he forgot to eat for days at a time.

To these examples of perseverance we can easily add the early Christians. The Acts of the Apostles, the second part of Luke's recounting of the good news, tells of a frightened group of apostles hiding in an upper room being transformed into courageous men and women who willingly died for their faith. The Spirit of God that descended on Pentecost showered many gifts on them that enabled them to witness to the risen Jesus and his gospel in the midst of an often hostile world. They continued to testify on the Lord's behalf first in Jerusalem, then in Judea and Samaria, and finally all over the Roman Empire and even in Rome itself.

## Perseverance

The dictionary defines *perseverance* as "the holding to a course of action, belief, or purpose without giving way; steadfastness." This quality is necessary for success at anything in life — studies, sports, a career, friendship, marriage, and the spiritual life.

Below are seven essential practices for personal and spiritual growth. Circle a number from 1 (very low) to 10 (very high) to rate your "stick-to-itiveness" in putting these into practice.

1. developing my own value system without conforming to peer pressure

   1 2 3 4 5 6 7 8 9 10

2. developing a steady practice of prayer or Bible reading

   1 2 3 4 5 6 7 8 9 10

3. speaking out for what I know is right without "wimping out"

   1 2 3 4 5 6 7 8 9 10

4. regularly meeting the Lord in the sacraments of the eucharist and reconciliation

   1 2 3 4 5 6 7 8 9 10

5. practicing patience with family members and classmates

   1 2 3 4 5 6 7 8 9 10

6. practicing acts of self-denial for the benefit of others

   1 2 3 4 5 6 7 8 9 10

7. trying to control my thoughts and actions in the area of sexual temptation

   1 2 3 4 5 6 7 8 9 10

## ▪ journal ▪

At the 18th Olympics in Tokyo, spectators could see the following words spelled out in lights:

> The most important thing in the Olympic Games is not to win but to take part; just as the most important thing in life is not the triumph but the struggle. The essential thing is. . .to have fought well.

Discuss whether you agree or disagree with this quote. Give reasons for your response. Give examples from your own life to support your argument.

## Author, Date, and Similarities to Luke's Gospel

In Chapter 6 we saw that Luke wrote both the gospel that bears his name and the Acts of the Apostles. He addressed them both to Theophilus. Their style and language are the same. Many scholars date Acts shortly after Luke's gospel, perhaps sometime in the mid–80s.

A close comparison of Acts to the gospel of Luke reveals many striking similarities, suggesting a common author. For example, their geographical emphasis is the same, the story lines are parallel, and they treat the same themes.

Recall the central role of Jerusalem in the gospel of Luke. As an infant and a child of twelve, Jesus traveled to Jerusalem. Later, he aimed his whole public ministry at "going up to Jerusalem" where the paschal mystery of God's love would take place. The resurrected Lord instructs his disciples to stay in Jerusalem and await the coming of the Holy Spirit.

Acts begins with an appearance of Jesus to the apostles before his ascension into heaven. At this meeting, Jesus tells them about their future mission: "But you will receive the power of the Holy Spirit which will come on you, and then you will be my witnesses not only in Jerusalem but throughout Judaea and Samaria, and indeed to earth's remotest end" (Acts 1:8).

Once again Jerusalem is central: It serves as the base of operations for the future growth of the church. Acts tells the story of the remarkable spread of Christianity from its small beginnings on Pentecost to every corner of the Roman world. It concludes with Paul in Rome itself, fearlessly teaching the good news to all who wished to hear.

Finally, several themes in the two works are alike. Two in particular stand out. First, *the Holy Spirit is active and alive in the disciples of Jesus,* continuing his work in the world.

In studying Luke, we saw how the Spirit led and directed Jesus. As you read Acts, note the central role of the Holy Spirit. From Jesus' promise to send the Spirit (Acts 1:5) to the outpouring of the Spirit (Acts 2:1–13) to the Spirit's powerful presence — enabling the apostles to preach, perform miracles, testify to the truth, settle disputes, persevere in their mission despite persecution, and witness to the end of the earth — the Spirit holds center stage in Acts. The Acts of the Apostles, which stresses the missionary activity of key "ambassadors for Christ," can rightfully be called the "Gospel of the Holy Spirit."

A second major theme emphasized in Acts is that *the gospel is for all people,* Jew and Gentile alike. Our study of Luke revealed that Jesus was the universal Messiah whose compassionate love embraced everyone. Likewise, a major turning point in Acts takes place when the Spirit inspires church leaders at a council in Jerusalem to allow Gentiles to convert to Christianity without first becoming Jews. Faith, baptism, and repentance — all gifts of Christ' love — are enough to receive the gospel and become part of the Lord's body. With this inspired decision, Christianity became a universal religion, open to everyone.

■ *discuss* ■

**Read Acts 2:42–47 and 4:32–35, which describe the early Christian community. Could the church today live like this? Why or why not? Would it be desirable for us to do so? Explain.**

## Prologue (Acts 1:1–11)

Luke uses the prologue to link the continuing story of salvation history in Acts to his earlier work. First, he addresses his work to Theophilus. Second, he tells his readers that the risen Jesus appeared to his disciples over a period of forty days. During this time, the Lord taught his disciples about their future vocation under the power of the Holy Spirit.

Luke probably chose the number forty to remind his readers how Yahweh remained with the Israelites for forty years in the desert. Forty also suggests the desert retreat of Jesus before he began his ministry. Luke's use of this symbolic number suggests a period of preparation for the disciples before the outpouring of the Holy Spirit.

Jesus' ascension marks the end of his appearances, a transition in salvation history from Jesus' earthly ministry to the age of the church. In turn, the era of the church will end on the day when Jesus "will come back in the same way."

# The Church in Jerusalem (Acts 1:12—5:42)

*Preparation for the Coming of the Spirit (1:15–26).* The first community of Christians included the apostles and other disciples of Jesus, including Mary his mother and several other women. Luke tells us that another ten days passed before the descent of the Holy Spirit. The expectant community prepared itself by praying, as Jesus had done so often.

During this period of prayer, the disciples chose Matthias to replace Judas, bringing the number of apostles back to twelve. The twelve apostles represent the twelve tribes of Israel. The church was to be the New Israel, the result of God's new covenant with all people. Matthias' qualifications for his new role as witness was that he was a close associate of Jesus during his entire public ministry.

*The Descent of the Holy Spirit (2:1–13).* The Hebrew scriptures often used the images of fire and wind to describe God's coming. Isaiah, for example, prophesied:

> For see how Yahweh comes in fire,. . .I am coming to gather every nation and every language. They will come to witness my glory (Is 66:15,18).

*Pentecost*, meaning "fiftieth," was a major Jewish feast occurring fifty days after Passover. It celebrated God's covenant with Moses; it was also a thanksgiving feast for the harvest of the previous year. Jews from all over the Mediterranean world traveled to Jerusalem for the festival. This explains why so many Jews of different languages were present in the holy city when Peter began his preaching.

On this glorious day, known as the birthday of the church, two miracles took place. First, the Holy Spirit inspired the apostles, giving them the courage to proclaim the gospel. Second, people from different countries understood the message in their own languages. This second miracle reversed the confusion that overtook the people building the Tower of Babel. Chapter 11 in the book of Genesis tells the story of a group of people who thought they could build a tower to heaven by their own efforts. God punished them for their pride by confusing the languages and scattering people all over the world (Gn 11:9). The birth of the church created a new human community under the power of the Spirit.

*Peter's Pentecost Homily (2:14–40; 3:11–26).* Acts contains eighteen sermons attributed to figures such as Peter, Paul, and Stephen. None is a word-for-word report of an actual talk. Rather, Luke drew on his written resources and the oral tradition to capture the spirit, style, content, and flavor of early sermons by the original witnesses to Jesus.

Perhaps the most famous sermon in Acts is Peter's Pentecost homily. It contains the *kerygma,* that is, the central proclamation of the gospel message — the life, death, and resurrection of Jesus. Most of the sermons in Acts follow a common pattern, outlined below.

1) *An introduction relates the speech to the rest of the story* (2:14–21). For example, Peter assures his audience that the disciples are not drunk, as some of the listeners assumed. He reminds them of Joel's prophecy that the Lord would pour out his Spirit on the people. The day of the Lord has arrived!

2) *An outline of the Jesus story uses Old Testament proofs to support the argument* (2:22–36). Peter's proclamation masterfully retells the life of Jesus. First he reports the many miracles Jesus performed, demonstrating God's reign working through him. Second, he tells how the people had Jesus crucified, a crime in which his hearers had their part to play. Third, he announces Jesus' glorious resurrection and ascension, as prophesied by David. He and the other apostles were eyewitnesses to these events. Fourth, he reports that Jesus kept his promise to send the Holy Spirit.

3) *The sermon issues a call for action: repentance and baptism* (2:37–40). The powerful words of the Holy Spirit, spoken through Peter, cut to the heart of those who heard them. They sincerely wanted to respond to the message they heard. Peter tells them they must repent and accept baptism in the Lord's name, after which they will receive the gift of the Holy Spirit. According to Acts, over three thousand joyously received Jesus as the "Lord and Christ" on this day.

**▪ journal ▪**

In Acts 3, Luke tells us that shortly after Pentecost, Peter gave a man crippled from birth the ability to walk. This was a gift that neither gold nor silver could buy. Peter bestowed it in the name of Jesus. As Jesus demonstrated the coming of the reign of God through miracles, so now the apostles also continue his preaching through powerful deeds.

This miracle gave Peter and John the attention of the crowd, enabling them to preach about Jesus.

Using the three points above, outline the elements of Peter's second sermon (Acts 3:11–26).

*Christian Community.* Luke describes how the early Christians lived (2:42–47). In these few verses, he depicts the characteristics of an ideal Christian community: *teaching, eucharist, prayer,* and *Christian fellowship.* A Christian community must take root in the gospel truth handed on by the apostles and their successors. Furthermore, Jesus' church must derive its nourishment from the eucharist and from spiritual communion with the Lord in prayer. Finally, Christians must live community — loving and caring for each other's needs. Teaching, eucharist, prayer, and sharing lead to joyful hearts united in the one Spirit.

---

## Christian Community

Analyze a Christian community you know something about — your school. How well does it live the four characteristics Luke sets down as the hallmarks of disciples of Christ? Rate your school according to this scale: **4** — excellent in showing this quality to **1** — very poor in putting this quality into practice.

____ *Teaching* (a sound religious education in the truths of the faith)

____ *Eucharist* (breaking bread in the Lord's name)

____ *Prayer* (seeking the Lord's help in everything)

____ *Sharing* (a caring community that looks out for others)

Discuss your ratings and suggest ways your school could improve.

---

*Before the Sanhedrin (4:1–31; 5:12–42).* Although Acts reports the extraordinary spread of Christianity, it also tells us that preaching about Jesus brought persecution to the early

Christians. To experience Jesus in his glory requires following Jesus in his suffering.

The first to oppose the apostles are the Sanhedrin, the Jewish ruling council. The first trial scene is typical:

1) The apostles perform a miracle that draws the attention of the crowd;

2) the apostles teach the crowds;

3) this teaching and popularity with the crowds draw the attention of the officials who arrest the apostles;

4) when put on trial, the apostles boldly defend themselves and proclaim Jesus even to their enemies;

5) a miraculous delivery from prison takes place, or the apostles are allowed to go free, and they continue their work of proclaiming the reign of God.

In this first brush with the authorities, although the apostles were warned not to preach Jesus' name again, they gathered and prayed to the Lord to "help your servants to proclaim your message with all fearlessness" (Acts 4:29). They performed more miracles, and many more people converted to Jesus. The high priest, encouraged by the Sadducees, arrested the apostles, but this time an angel miraculously freed them.

After their miraculous rescue, the apostles refused to go underground. Rather, they began preaching openly again in the Temple. When the high priest heard of this, he arrested them once again. Peter and the apostles eloquently defended themselves. In the process, they infuriated the Sadducees so much that they wanted to put the apostles to death. However, Gamaliel, a Pharisee and a wise member of the council, offered excellent advice:

> "Leave these men alone and let them go. If this enterprise, this movement of theirs, is of human origin it will break up of its own accord; but if it does in fact come from God you will be unable to destroy them. Take care not to find yourselves fighting against God" (Acts 5:38–39).

The leaders agreed with the soundness of Gamaliel's advice; however, they flogged the apostles and warned them never to speak in the name of Jesus again. The apostles rejoiced that they had preached Jesus name even though they suffered for it, and they ignored the warning, proclaiming the gospel in the Temple as well in private homes around Jerusalem.

### ▪ journal ▪

The Sanhedrin commanded the apostles *never* to speak of Jesus again, but the apostles felt that they simply had to ignore that warning. Reflect on these questions.

If the civil authorities commanded you never to speak about Jesus, would you obey? If yes, why? If no, why not?

### ▪ discuss ▪

**"Christians today are too lukewarm in their faith to suffer for Jesus." Do you agree or disagree?**

### ▪ research ▪

**If possible, interview a permanent deacon. Find out what his duties are.**

## Witness in Judea and Samaria (Acts 6:1—12:25)

After reading the first part of Acts and its description of the first Christian community, you might conclude that early Christians lived constantly in unity, peace, joy, and love. Although Luke paints an idealistic portrait of the early church, he also shows some of its flaws.

For example, Luke tells us that the Greek-speaking Jewish-Christians in Jerusalem felt their widows were not being treated fairly in the daily distribution of food. They felt that the Aramaic-speaking Jews from Palestine were prejudiced against them.

To resolve this crisis, the apostles appointed seven deacons (from the Greek work *diakonia,* meaning *service*) to oversee the daily tasks of the community such as the distribution of food to those in need. The particular vocation of the apostles was to lead others in prayer and to witness to the word of God. By appointing deacons, they created a new ministry in the church.

This is a striking parallel to today's church with its many needs. In recent years various ministries (for example, eucharistic minister, youth minister, minister to the sick) have come into existence as a result of the renewal in the church brought about by Vatican II. In addition, the permanent diaconate itself has been revived. The Spirit is guiding the church today just as it did in the earliest days of Christianity.

*Trial and Death of Stephen (6:8—8:3).* Stephen is the best known of the first seven deacons. He performed many miracles and eloquently proclaimed the gospel. So convincing was his preaching that the Sanhedrin brought him to trial and accused him of blasphemy. Stephen's accusations that his audience had conspired to murder Jesus infuriated them.

They drove him from the city and stoned him to death. Stephen, like his Lord, died forgiving his persecutors. Stephen is the first Christian *martyr*, a word meaning witness. He surrendered all he had for Christ.

Stephen's death precipitated a general persecution of Christians in Jerusalem. This caused many Christians to flee Jerusalem, which turned out to be a blessing in disguise, because they began to preach the gospel throughout Judea and even into Samaria. The early church was beginning to realize that the gospel should be offered to everyone.

■ *journal* ■

Acts reports that early Christians were jailed, tortured, stoned, and beheaded for following the Way. Christians today, at least in North America, are not treated in such extreme ways. They do, however, have to defend their faith against more subtle abuse. Write of a time when you suffered because of your Christian faith. What to you is the most difficult part of having the name *Christian*?

*Philip (8:4–40).* Philip, one of the significant missionaries leaving Jerusalem, began to preach "the Christ" to the Samaritans. He also performed many miracles, as Jesus had promised his disciples would. The Samaritans, outcasts in the eyes of pious Jews, embraced the gospel with enthusiasm.

While in Samaria, Philip met a magician named Simon, referred to by his fellow Samaritans as Simon Magus (the "Great"). However, even Simon realized that his manipulation of unknown forces paled in comparison to the power of the Holy Spirit. He, too, accepted baptism and became a disciple of Philip.

Peter and John, hearing of Philip's success, came to Samaritan territory to lay hands on the newly baptized. Luke tells us that the newly baptized Samaritans had not received the Holy Spirit. Through a second ritual of praying for the coming of the Spirit and the imposition of hands, the gifts of the Spirit were bestowed on them. Today, we can see obvious parallels between this rite and the sacrament of confirmation.

Simon Magus was once again amazed at this further demonstration and offered to buy the power of God's gifts. Peter strongly rebuked him and ordered him to repent, saying that

God's gifts are freely given. Simon accepted the rebuke and prayed for forgiveness. Today the sin of *simony*, the buying of spiritual benefits, bears his name.

Philip has another opportunity to preach the gospel, this time to an Ethiopian eunuch in Judea. This Ethiopian, because he was castrated, was an outcast under Jewish Law, but he had a genuine interest in God and the Jewish religion. When Philip carefully explained the meaning of the prophecies of Isaiah concerning Jesus, the Ethiopian believed and requested baptism. The gospel was indeed starting to move beyond Jerusalem.

*Paul's Conversion (9:1–30).* One of the most fortunate events for Christianity was Saul's blinding vision of Jesus on the road to Damascus. Saul, known as Paul in Greek, was on his way to persecute Christians in the city of Damascus when he was knocked from his horse by a flash of light and a voice that said, "Saul, Saul, why are persecuting me?" The voice went on to say: "I am Jesus, whom you are persecuting" (9:5).

Because he was now blind, his companions led him into the city, where a Christian named Ananias healed him. Paul was a changed man. He believed, was baptized, and began to preach so powerfully in all the synagogues that the Jewish authorities tried to kill him. Fleeing to Jerusalem, Paul had a hard time convincing the Christians of his radical change. Eventually Barnabas befriended him, introduced him to the apostles, and told them of Jesus' appearance to him. Paul was accepted by the community and began to preach boldly in the name of the Lord. However, he angered some Greek-speaking Jews who began to plot his death. Paul escaped to Tarsus, his hometown, where he remained for many months, prayerfully preparing for his later ministry.

*Cornelius' Baptism: Gentile Pentecost (10:1—11:18).* Chapter 10 of Acts tells us how God revealed his will through the dreams of the Gentile centurion Cornelius and the apostle Peter. Peter's dream indicated that God's salvation embraced all people, Gentile as well as Jew. Cornelius' dream told him to send for Peter. Peter began his speech to Cornelius' household in words that would change the future of Christianity: "I now really understand. . . that God has no favorites, but that anybody of any nationality who fears him and does what is right is acceptable to him" (10:34–35).

Peter told his Gentile audience about Jesus and his gospel. As he was speaking, the Spirit descended on all the listeners. This event rightfully bears the name the "Gentile Pentecost." On that day, Peter baptized Cornelius and his entire household. The gospel had entered the Gentile world through the power of the Spirit.

When Peter got back to Jerusalem, however, he had to defend his actions of associating with non-Jews. When Peter told of his dream, his fellow Jewish-Christians accepted that God had indeed extended his salvation to all people.

■ *project* ■

**Early Christians cared for each other by responding to each other's needs. For example, the church in Antioch took up a collection for the starving in Judea (Acts 11:29–30). As a class, devise a service project and raise at least $100 for a homeless shelter or soup kitchen in your city.**

## Witness to the Ends of the Earth (Acts 13:1—28:31)

*Paul's First Missionary Journey (13:1—15:35).* The year 45 marks a turning point in the early history of the church. In that year Paul, joined by Barnabas, began extensive missionary activity into the Gentile world. This first journey took Paul to Cyprus and into Asia Minor, from Seleucia to Salamas and from there to Paphos. The trip also included Perga in Pamphylia, the towns of Lycaonia and a return through Lystra, Iconium, Antioch in Pisidia, Perga, the port of Attalia, and Antioch in Syria.

The names of these cities sound strange to us. What did Paul and Barnabas do there? They first went to the Jewish synagogues to preach the gospel to the Jews who had been living there as part of what is known as the Diaspora. This technical term refers to the dispersion of Jewish people to the areas outside of Palestine during the first century B.C. These Jewish communities throughout the Mediterranean area gave the early Christian missionaries points of contact on their travels.

An example of the preaching they did is Paul's long speech in Antioch in Pisidia. In his proclamation, Paul reviewed key events of salvation history and the many promises God made to his people. Then he recounted the death and resurrection of Jesus and proclaimed forgiveness of sin in Jesus' name. Sometimes, like in this city of Antioch, the missionaries' words fell on receptive ears. At other times, though, their preaching about Christ was rejected by the established Jewish communities, who threw the missionaries out of the synagogues and often hounded them out of the cities.

Paul and his companions then began to preach to the Gentiles, many of whom embraced the gospel. Paul justified this shift in these words:

> "We had to proclaim the word of God to you first, but since you have rejected it. . .here and now we turn to the gentiles. For this is what the Lord commanded us to do when he said:
>
> 'I have made you a light to the nations, so that my salvation may reach the remotest parts of the earth'" (Acts 13:46–47).

*Crisis in Jerusalem (15:1–35).* Some Jewish-Christians were upset that Paul and Barnabas were not requiring Gentile converts to submit to Jewish Law before baptism. This controversy resulted in a meeting in Jerusalem around the year 49, at which the leaders decided the question on behalf of freedom for the Gentiles. Peter reminded the assembly that he himself had witnessed the outpouring of the Spirit on the Gentiles. The grace of the Lord Jesus saves, not adherence to the Law. Paul and Barnabas described in detail all the signs and wonders God's grace was working among the Gentiles to whom they preached.

James also spoke at this assembly and agreed that Gentile-Christians should be free of most of the restrictions of the Law. The exceptions were few: avoid anything associated with the worship of false gods (idolatry), meat that Jewish Law considered unclean, and marriages considered incestuous under Jewish Law. These restrictions helped smooth relations with Jewish-Christians brought up in the Law. The assembly drafted a letter for Paul and Barnabas and two other companions to read to the church in Antioch.

*Second Missionary Journey (15:36—18:23).* Paul's second journey took him to many of the cities to which he subsequently wrote his letters: Thessalonica, Philippi, Corinth, and Ephesus. It also took him to Athens, the heart of the ancient Greek world. Paul, along with his companions Silas and Timothy, preached from town to town. In Troas Paul had a vision of a man from Macedonia, in Europe, begging him to come to help them. Paul changed his initial plans and decided to head for Philippi, the principal city in Macedonia.

**discuss**

**Suppose the pope asked your help in drawing up an agenda for a council to be called next year with the theme "Important Issues Facing a 21st-Century Church." In your opinion, what three problems or challenges should the council address? What solutions would you propose?**

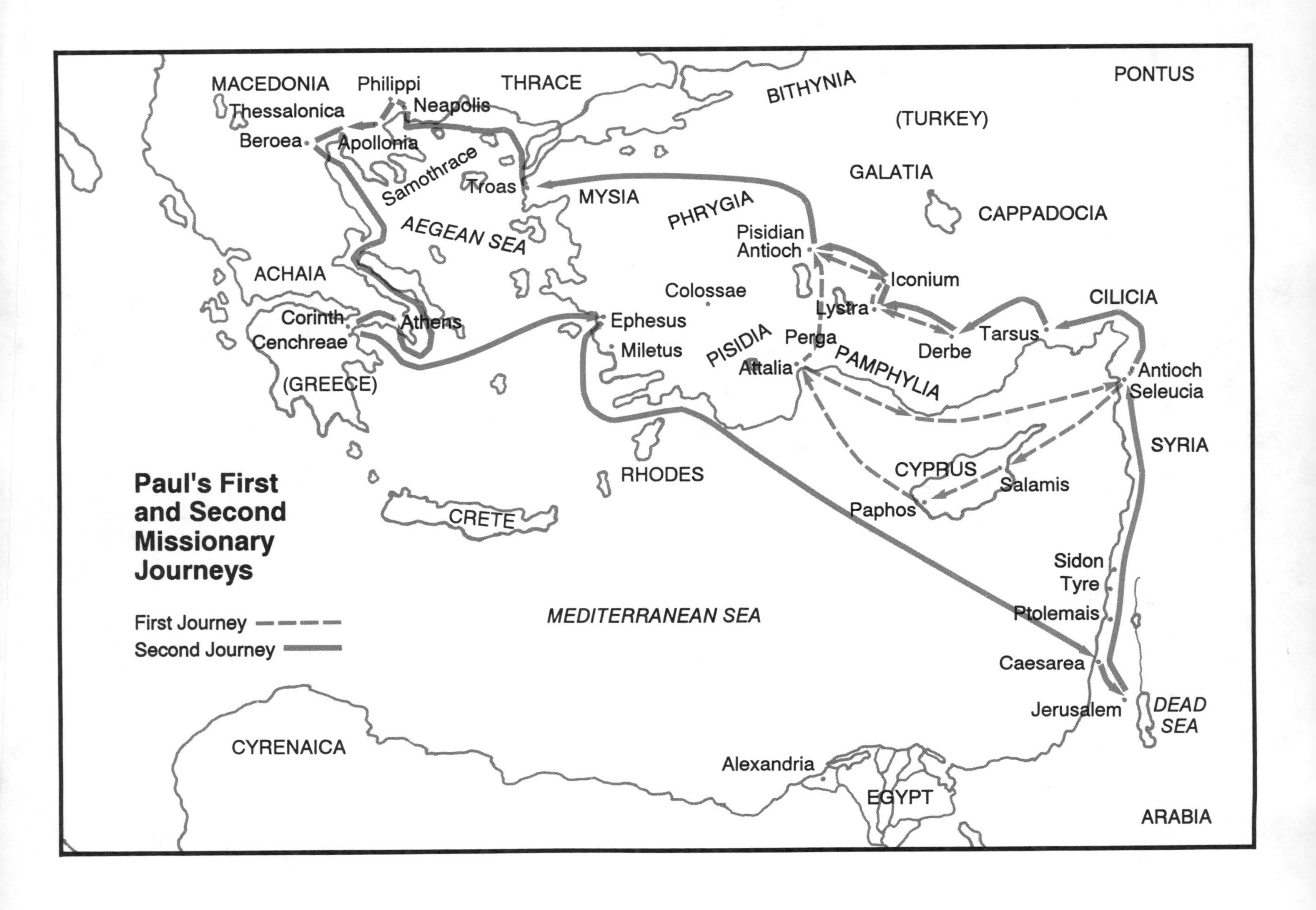
Paul's First and Second Missionary Journeys
First Journey
Second Journey
MACEDONIA
Philippi
THRACE
Thessalonica
Neapolis
Beroea
Apollonia
Samothrace
Troas
AEGEAN SEA
ACHAIA
Corinth
Cenchreae
Athens
(GREECE)
CRETE
RHODES
BITHYNIA
(TURKEY)
PONTUS
GALATIA
CAPPADOCIA
MYSIA
PHRYGIA
Pisidian Antioch
Iconium
Colossae
Lystra
Ephesus
Miletus
PISIDIA
Perga
Attalia
PAMPHYLIA
Derbe
Tarsus
CILICIA
Antioch
Seleucia
SYRIA
CYPRUS
Salamis
Paphos
Sidon
Tyre
Ptolemais
Caesarea
Jerusalem
DEAD SEA
MEDITERRANEAN SEA
CYRENAICA
Alexandria
EGYPT
ARABIA

At first, he had success preaching to Lydia, the wealthy owner of a lucrative purple-dye trade. She converted to Christianity, along with all the members of her household, and she opened her home to the missionaries.

After this success, the missionaries got into trouble when they cured a possessed slave girl who made money for her owners by telling fortunes. Paul and Silas were arrested and charged as troublemakers. After being flogged, they were thrown in prison. Refusing to flee when an earthquake threw open their prison doors, Paul and Silas preached to the jailer, converting him and his family.

Paul's experiences in Thessalonica and Beroea repeated what happened in Philippi. At first, he was successful, even converting some prominent citizens. But this led to jealousy among the Jews, who charged Paul and Silas with disturbing the peace and being traitors to Rome. Eventually they were forced to move on, but troublemakers pursued them from city to city, stirring up the people against them.

In Athens, Paul had the opportunity to explain Christian faith to the cultured people of the city. Athenians worshipped many idols in temples around the city. They also engaged in deep philosophical arguments.

Paul tried to appeal to the basic religious sense of the Athenians. He especially singled out an altar they had erected to an "unknown God." Even the Greeks acknowledged there might be a god who was superior to all their gods and philosophies. Paul said: "In fact, the unknown God you revere is the one I proclaim to you" (17:23).

Using clever arguments, Paul showed how the God of Jesus was the invisible, all-present creator and sustainer of the universe. This true God, Paul went on, has made us all his children. However, because God is almighty and spiritual, it is foolish to think we can represent the deity in the form of an idol. An open-minded Athenian of Paul's day could probably accept this teaching, and several did, although others ridiculed him for the Christian belief in resurrection.

*journal*

**Paul eloquently presented the Christian faith to the Athenians. Suppose you had to speak to a group of atheists. Outline five major points you would include in your talk.**

Paul's next stop was in Corinth where he took up residence with Aquila and his wife Priscilla. Corinth was a Greek port city with its share of both wealthy merchants and a poor underclass: prostitutes, criminals, gamblers. Paul earned a living in Corinth by making tents. On the Sabbath, he preached in the synagogues. When Silas and Timothy joined him from Macedonia, Paul proclaimed the gospel every day. He successfully convinced a president of the synagogue, Crispus, and his family to accept Jesus. But many other Jews opposed him. Some took him to the Roman governor who let him go free because he thought Paul was involved in a simple religious dispute with the Jews.

Paul remained in Corinth for a year and a half and helped to build the Christian community there before he decided it was time to return to Antioch. On the way, he stayed briefly in Ephesus but promised to return later.

■ *discuss* ■

**Paul's ministry reminds us that some occupations are contrary to Christian belief and practice. List five modern professions or jobs that a Christian of conscience simply should not do. Give reasons for your choices.**

*Third Missionary Journey (18:24—21:14).* Ephesus was the most important city in Paul's third missionary effort, which probably began around 54. He spent two years there instructing other preachers such as Apollos. He also conferred the Spirit, preached in the synagogues, performed exorcisms, and proclaimed the gospel to the citizens. Paul was successful enough that the sales of silver miniatures of a famous pagan goddess in Ephesus were greatly reduced. This angered a leading silversmith, Demetrius, who incited a riotous meeting against Paul. The mob dispersed without any significant incident, but once again Paul felt he had to move on because he was endangering the lives of his converts.

Panoramic view of Ephesus.

Paul's next stop was Troas. Luke tells us that he met Paul at Troas and that he remained there for five days. Luke also records a startling event that took place in Troas:

> On the first day of the week we met for the breaking of bread. Paul was due to leave the next day, and he preached a sermon that went on till the middle of the night. A number of lamps were lit in the upstairs room where we were assembled, and as Paul went on and on, a young man called Eutychus who was sitting on the window-sill grew drowsy and was overcome by sleep and fell to the ground three floors below. He was picked up dead. Paul went down and stooped to clasp the boy to him, saying "There is no need to worry, there is still life in him." Then he went back upstairs where he broke the bread and ate and carried on talking till he left at daybreak. They took the boy away alive, and were greatly encouraged (Acts 20:7–12).

This story captures for us how the early Christians celebrated eucharist. They met at a Christian's house on the

Lord's Day and shared a fellowship meal. They broke bread in Jesus' name, and Christian instruction played a key role in the celebration.

After their short stay in Troas, Paul, Luke, and their companions went to Miletus. From there Paul would sail to Jerusalem and the exciting events connected with his imprisonment, various trials, and perilous trip to Rome.

## Research and Reflection

Reread Paul's farewell discourse to the elders from Ephesus (Acts 20:17–38). Answer these questions:

1. How does Paul know that persecution is in store for him?
2. Who are the fierce wolves that might try to devour the new Christians when Paul is gone?
3. Paul quotes Jesus as saying, "There is more happiness in giving than in receiving." Give several examples in which you have found this to be true.

*From Jerusalem to Rome (21:15—28:31).* Paul no sooner arrived at Jerusalem than his Jewish enemies saw him and incited a riot against him. They charged him with speaking against the Law and the Temple, as well as profaning the Temple by bringing a Gentile into it. The crowd in the Temple dragged Paul out and began to beat him. But when the tribune got word of it, he arrested Paul and took him to the fortress. When he heard of a plot to kill Paul, he removed him under heavy guard to Caesarea. There, the Roman procurator Felix kept him under house arrest for two years.

In the meantime, the Roman procurator Festus succeeded Felix and inherited the problem of Paul. In a visit to Jerusalem, Festus heard all the false charges the Sanhedrin made against Paul. To ingratiate himself with the Jewish leaders, he proposed taking Paul before the Sanhedrin. Paul, however, knew he would not get a fair trial in Jerusalem and invoked his right as a Roman citizen to a trial in one of Caesar's courts in Rome. Festus agreed.

Acts concludes rather abruptly. The authorities put Paul under house arrest around 61. Paul had considerable freedom during his two-year arrest in Rome. He spent some of

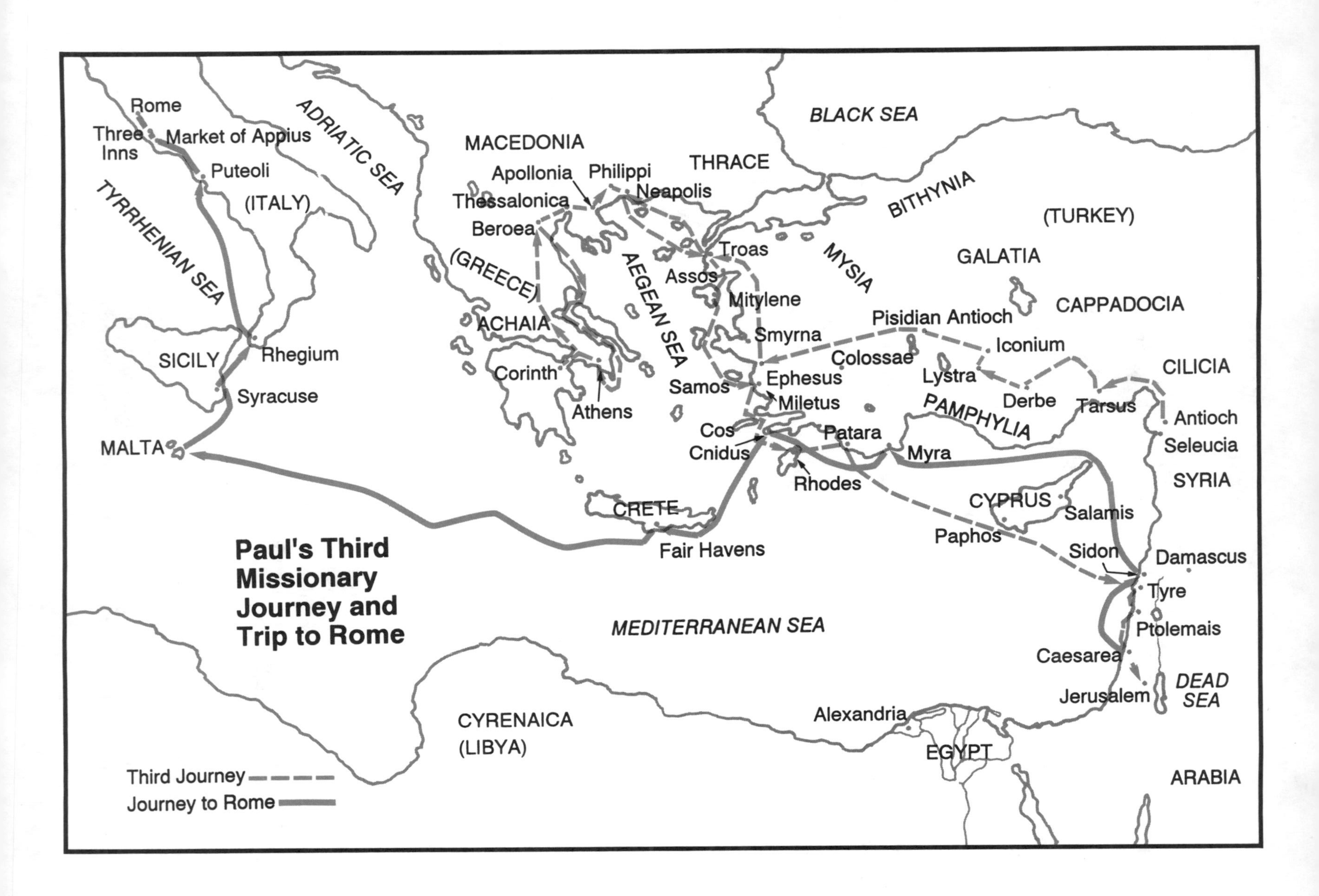
Paul's Third Missionary Journey and Trip to Rome
Third Journey
Journey to Rome
Rome
Three Inns
Market of Appius
Puteoli
ADRIATIC SEA
(ITALY)
TYRRHENIAN SEA
SICILY
Rhegium
Syracuse
MALTA
MACEDONIA
Apollonia
Philippi
Neapolis
Thessalonica
Beroea
(GREECE)
ACHAIA
Corinth
Athens
AEGEAN SEA
THRACE
BLACK SEA
BITHYNIA
(TURKEY)
MYSIA
Troas
Assos
Mitylene
Smyrna
Ephesus
Samos
Miletus
Cos
Cnidus
Rhodes
Patara
Myra
GALATIA
CAPPADOCIA
Pisidian Antioch
Iconium
Colossae
Lystra
Derbe
CILICIA
Tarsus
PAMPHYLIA
Antioch
Seleucia
SYRIA
CYPRUS
Salamis
Paphos
CRETE
Fair Havens
Sidon
Damascus
Tyre
Ptolemais
Caesarea
Jerusalem
DEAD SEA
MEDITERRANEAN SEA
CYRENAICA
(LIBYA)
Alexandria
EGYPT
ARABIA

his time meeting with Jewish leaders, trying to explain how the Hebrew scriptures pointed to Jesus and how they even prophesied a mission to the Gentiles. Luke ends his work this way:

> He [Paul] spent the whole of the two years in his own rented lodging. He welcomed all who came to visit him, proclaiming the kingdom of God and teaching the truth about the Lord Jesus Christ with complete fearlessness and without any hindrance from anyone (Acts 28:30–31).

Christian tradition holds that Paul was eventually condemned and beheaded in Rome in the year 67. Instead of ending his two-volume work on the sad note of Paul's death, however, Luke hints at a third work — the "Acts of Christians." The Spirit remains alive. Despite opposition, Christians must continue to do what Paul did — proclaim the gospel of God's compassionate love in Jesus Christ until the end of time. Thus, Luke's ending is joyful and challenging. Now it is up to us to put into action the teachings of Jesus and the preaching of the apostles.

## ▪ focus questions ▪

1. How do we know that Luke wrote Acts?
2. Discuss several ways the Holy Spirit takes center stage in Acts.
3. Why did Luke write Acts?
4. Why do the apostles choose someone to replace Judas?
5. Explain the significance of the Holy Spirit coming on the Jewish feast of Pentecost.
6. What are the main points of a typical sermon in Acts?
7. How does Acts describe the ideal Christian community?
8. What advice did Gamaliel give concerning the early Christian community?
9. Why did the early church first appoint deacons?
10. What event precipitated Christian preaching outside Jerusalem?
11. Identify Simon Magus.

12. Discuss the significance of Philip's conversion of an Ethiopian eunuch and Peter's conversion of Cornelius.
13. Describe Paul's conversion.
14. Discuss the meaning of one major dream recorded in Acts.
15. Discuss one significant event in *each* of Paul's missionary journeys.
16. What was so important about the Council of Jerusalem?
17. Explain a possible meaning for the way Luke ends Acts.
18. *Identify*:

| | |
|---|---|
| Barnabas | Matthias |
| Felix | Philip |
| James, son of Zebedee | Silas |
| James, brother of the Lord (Acts 12:17; Gal 1:19) | Stephen |
| | Timothy |

## ▪ vocabulary

**Copy the meaning of these words into your journal.**

**adherence**

**lucrative**

## ▪ exercise ▪

Read Luke's account of the shipwreck Paul experienced on his way to Rome, Acts 27:9–44. Note how the crew jettisoned its cargo to try to survive. Note, too, how non-swimmers clung to planks to help them make it to land once the ship hit the shoal.

Christians sometimes use an image of a storm-tossed ship on an angry sea to describe certain periods in their own lives. Reflect on your life to find a time you might describe this way.

Name three things in your life that are excess baggage, pulling you down, keeping you from smooth sailing (example: paying the price of popularity).

1. ______________________________

2. ______________________________

3. ______________________________

What one spiritual reality must you cling to absolutely in order to weather all storms that come your way? (example: the love of a friend)

______________________________

In your journal, discuss the steps you should take to rid yourself of the "excess cargo" that keeps you from being an outstanding disciple of Christ.

## Prayer Reflection

Acts is rightly called the Gospel of the Holy Spirit. Pray the following prayer to the Holy Spirit.

> Lord our God, you call us out of darkness into light,
> out of self-deception into truth,
> out of death into life.
> Send us your Holy Spirit
> to open our ears to your call.
> Fill our hearts with courage
> to be true followers of your Son.
>
> We ask this through Christ our Lord. Amen.

### ■ *reflection* ■

Who or what is calling you to respond to the Lord in your life? Are you open to the call?

### ■ *resolution* ■

Throughout the coming weeks, ask the Holy Spirit to give you the courage to do what you know is right. The Spirit is the source of courage and perseverance.

# *chapter* 9
# The Letters of St. Paul

The Apostle Paul—Rembrandt

Be vigilant, stay firm in the faith, be brave and strong. Let everything you do be done in love.

— 1 Corinthians 16:13–14

**In This Chapter**

We will study:

- Paul's own letters
- letters ascribed to Paul

A church in a large American city has as its slogan:

> "Wake up, sing up, preach up, pray up and pay up, but never give up or let up or back up or shut up until the cause of Christ in this church and in the world is built up."

It would not be surprising if this church was named St. Paul's — this slogan certainly applies to the apostle to the Gentiles. Paul's zeal for Jesus enabled the gospel to take root throughout the Roman Empire.

Paul was born around the year 10 in Tarsus, a city in Cilicia. He was a strict Jew of the tribe of Benjamin and received an excellent Greek education. He probably also learned to be a tentmaker there, an occupation he often used to support himself during his later missionary activity. As we read in Acts, Paul was also a Roman citizen, an important fact that spared him a beating in Jerusalem and ultimately led him to Rome for his trial.

Luke tells us that as a young man Paul studied to be a rabbi in Jerusalem under the famous teacher Gamaliel. Paul was a strict Pharisee, trained in the Law. He was among the leaders who persecuted the early Christians for deviating from true Jewish practice.

Recall from your reading of Acts Paul's dramatic conversion on the road to Damascus. The glorified Lord spoke to Paul in a blinding light, identifying himself with the Christians Paul was persecuting. This took place around the year 36. Paul was baptized by Ananias and then spent some time in the Arabian desert before returning to Damascus.

In the year 39, Paul left Damascus and went to Jerusalem to meet Peter and James and other leading disciples. He returned to a city in Cilicia, perhaps Tarsus, and remained there for around four years. Around 44 Barnabas came to ask Paul to help him minister in Antioch. After working there for a year, the Antioch church sent Paul and Barnabas to Jerusalem to help the Christians of Judea during a time of famine.

Between 46 and 58 Paul engaged in three extensive missionary journeys. On a return to Jerusalem in 58 his enemies had him arrested. After two years detainment in Caesarea, he finally made it to Rome around 61, where he was under house arrest for two more years. During his second and third missionary journeys and while under arrest in Rome, Paul wrote letters (epistles) to churches he had already visited or planned to visit. He also addressed some letters to individuals to instruct them in good Christian ministry.

## The Challenge of Paul

You can't read Paul without hearing the challenge of growing in the Christian life. Carefully and prayerfully read Romans 12. Then examine yourself on the following checklist. Use the following scale: **1** — I've shown a lot of growth on this; **2** — I am making some progress; **3** — I'm stagnant.

| | 1 | 2 | 3 |
|---|---|---|---|
| 1. "Do not model your behavior on the contemporary world." | | | |
| 2. "Never pride yourself on being better than you really are." | | | |
| 3. "In the service of the Lord, work. . . with an eager spirit." | | | |
| 4. "Look for opportunities to be hospitable." | | | |
| 5. "Be at peace with everyone." | | | |

### ■ *exercise* ■

Paul discusses many qualities of Christian love in these verses from Romans. But remember that he does so within the context of a letter. With the convenience of the telephone, we in the twentieth century may be losing the art of letter writing. Yet, we all like to *receive* letters because we can read them again and again and they remind us of our loved ones.

Why not take Paul's advice and spread your love to someone you really care for? Write a letter to a grandparent or a friend who has moved away or to a brother or sister in college. Besides sharing personal news, be sure to tell the person what he or she means to you.

The New Testament contains twenty-one epistles, thirteen of which were either written by or attributed to Paul. These letters are not listed in chronological order in our Bibles. Rather, they are arranged in two groups: letters to communities and letters to individuals. Within each group, they appear from the longest to the shortest. Letters to a community, and probably letters to individuals as well, were read and reflected on by the entire community.

*Did Paul Write All These Letters?* Scholars agree that Paul wrote at least seven of the thirteen letters attributed to him: Romans, 1 and 2 Corinthians, 1 Thessalonians, Galatians, Philippians, and Philemon. The others — 2 Thessalonians, Ephesians, Colossians, 1 and 2 Timothy, and Titus — might have been written by close disciples of Paul. The teaching in these six letters is certainly *Pauline,* that is, similar in style and content to what Paul consistently taught in his other letters. Paul's disciples used his name to gain authority for their own teaching, an accepted practice in the ancient world.

This recognition that not all thirteen letters which bear Paul's name are actually written by him is a finding of contemporary scripture scholarship. Traditionally, all were believed to have been written by Paul and this is the way they are still presented in the church's liturgy. The lectionary, which contains all of the Bible readings for the liturgy, introduces all Pauline letters with the words, "A reading from the letter of Paul to the ...."

It has also been traditional to group certain of Paul's letters together based on their themes or place of writing. For example, Philippians, Colossians, Philemon, and Ephesians are sometimes called "prison letters" or "captivity letters" because Paul, or the author writing in his name, wrote these while in captivity. Another traditional category has been called the "pastoral letters": Titus and 1 and 2 Timothy. These letters are addressed to disciples of Paul whom he appointed as bishops for certain churches. They focus on the role of Timothy and Titus as "pastors" and are concerned with church organization and purity of faith.

## Pauline Letters[1]

### Paul's Own Letters

| Letter | Date | Place Where Written |
|---|---|---|
| 1 Thessalonians | 50 or 51 | Corinth |
| Galatians | 54 | Ephesus |
| 1 Corinthians | 54 | Ephesus |
| 2 Corinthians[2] | 55 | Macedonia (either Thessalonica or Philippi) and Illyricum |
| Philemon | 56 or 57 | Ephesus |
| Philippians[3] | 57 and 58 | Ephesus |
| Romans | 57 or 58 | Corinth |

### Letters Ascribed to Paul[4]

| Letter | Date | Place Where Written |
|---|---|---|
| Colossians | 70s | Ephesus |
| Ephesians | 80 to 100 | Ephesus |
| 2 Thessalonians | 90s | Asia Minor |
| Titus, 1 and 2 Timothy | about 100 | Asia Minor |

▪ *journal* ▪

**Read the addresses of any six of Paul's letters. Record in your journal the Christian way of greeting.**

*Style.* Paul's letters follow the common style of letter-writing of his day. His letters contain four sections:

1. *Opening Address.* Since the letters were not placed in

[1] Information in this chart is based on the *New Jerome Biblical Commentary.*

[2] 2 Corinthians is today recognized as a compilation of at least two letters which scholars believe Paul wrote in the spring and fall of 55 from what is today Greece and Yugoslavia.

[3] Like 2 Corinthians, many scholars believe that Philippians as we have it today is a compilation of three separate letters. The first two were probably written near the end of Paul's stay in Ephesus and the third shortly thereafter.

[4] These dates and places represent the best guess of contemporary scholars.

envelopes, the opening salutation gives the name of the sender and the receiver and a short greeting.

2. *Thanksgiving*. A short thanksgiving sets the tone of the letter and hints at the letter's contents. Paul's thanksgivings are usually very prayerful and inspiring.

3. *Body of the letter*. The bulk of the letter has two parts to it: 1) *doctrinal teaching* — Paul elaborates key Christian truths or clarifies misunderstandings his readers are having over points of Christian doctrine; 2) *encouragement* — Paul applies the doctrinal teaching to Christian living. Today, we look to these sections of Paul's letters for guidance in Christian morality.

4. *Final salutations*. Paul concludes by giving personal news or specific advice to individuals. His final greeting is usually a short blessing such as, "The grace of our Lord Jesus Christ be with you" (1 Thes 5:28).

You might notice a conclusion such as this in some of Paul's letters: "This greeting is in my own hand — PAUL" (1 Cor 16:21). This verse tells us that Paul dictated his letters to a professional scribe, a common practice in his day. Toward the end of the letter he would sign his name to assure his readers that the letter was really coming from him.

## Sampling Paul

St. Paul is one of the outstanding Christian theologians of all time. His teachings are fundamental to understanding the meaning of salvation history, the role of Jesus, the church, and life in the Spirit. Even today, Paul's instructions on prayer, Christian living, and church administration give us much food for thought as we try to adapt the biblical word to the contemporary world.

Below are eight summary statements that capture the essence of Paul's rich teaching. Study them carefully. Then read the passage listed. These passages are among the best known and most important in all of Paul's writings. For each reading, note in your journal several significant points Paul makes in that particular passage.

1. Salvation takes place through Jesus Christ, the Lord of the universe (Col 1:15–20).
2. The heart of the gospel is the death and resurrection of Jesus (1 Cor 15:1–19).

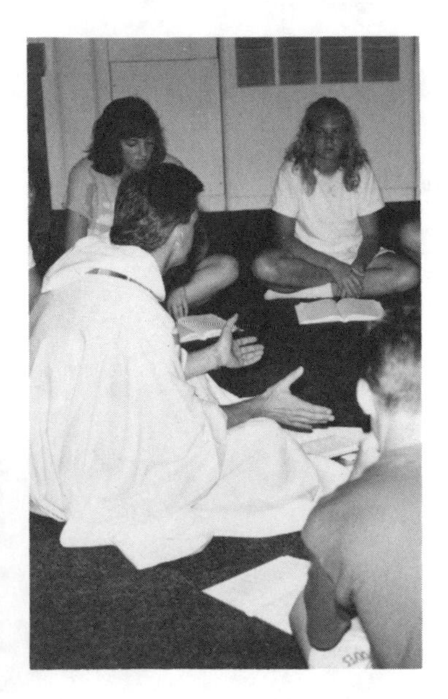

3. Christians will participate in the resurrection of Jesus Christ (1 Cor 15:20–28).
4. Salvation is a free gift from God that demands faith. We cannot earn it (Rom 5:1–11).
5. Christians are bound together in one body, the church, of which Jesus is the head (1 Cor 12:12–30).
6. The Holy Spirit is the life of the church who enables us to call God Abba (Gal 4:1–7).
7. The brothers and sisters of Jesus should treat each other with dignity. We must love (Eph 4:17–32).
8. Following Jesus means that we must suffer for him gladly (Phil 2:1–18).

## Paul's Own Letters

*1 Thessalonians.* During his second missionary journey, Paul visited Thessalonica, an important commercial center and capital of the Roman province of Macedonia, in the summer of 50. Along with his coworkers Timothy and Silas, Paul made converts among both the Jews and the Gentiles until some of the Jews turned on him and drove him from the city. Paul went to Beroea, then to Athens, and eventually to Corinth, where he remained for many months.

While Paul was in Corinth, Timothy had visited the Thessalonians to encourage them in their faith. Timothy returned to Paul with the good news that the Thessalonians were remaining faithful under persecution. However, Paul wanted to address a couple of issues — what happens to Christians after death and specific instructions in Christian living. Probably in the winter of 50–51 Paul wrote his first letter.

The outline of this letter follows the typical style of an epistle. Note the four sections: opening address (1:1); thanksgiving (1:2–10); body of the letter (2:1—5:22) — Paul reviews his previous relations with the Thessalonians and offers thanks (2:1—3:13) and gives specific instructions and encouragement to the community (4:1—5:22); conclusion (5:23–28).

Read 1 Thessalonians. Note how in the second part of the body of the letter (4:1—5:22), Paul takes up some issues that were troubling the Thessalonians. First, Paul reminds his

readers of their vocation to holiness. He warns them especially against sexual immorality and calls them to grow in Christian love for each other. Second, he tells them not to worry about their brothers and sisters who have already died. They, too, will rise and join Christ in glory when he comes again. Paul tells his readers to be always ready for the time of Jesus' return.

The letter concludes joyfully with Paul encouraging his friends to live at peace and in unity.

*Galatians.* Along with 1 and 2 Corinthians and Romans, Galatians is sometimes called one of the "great letters" because of its deep theological insights and timeless practical advice on Christian living.

Paul wrote it to a group of churches in Iconium, Derbe, and Lystra — cities in the Roman province of Galatia. He visited this area on both his second and third missionary journeys. Most scholars believe this letter was written in 54 or 55, during Paul's lengthy stay in Ephesus.

Galatians is an angry, almost unfriendly letter. Paul wrote it to counteract a group known as *Judaizers*, Jewish-Christian missionaries who followed him into Galatia. They began to teach Paul's converts that they had to keep certain precepts of the Mosaic Law in addition to believing in Christ. They also questioned Paul's authority to teach, claiming that Paul should have circumcised his new converts.

Although Galatians has an address (1:1–5) and a conclusion (6:11–18), nowhere does Paul thank his readers for their spiritual condition. They had not yet proven their faith and, in fact, were showing themselves easily led by false teachers. Instead, Paul warns his readers about following a different gospel than he preached (1:6–10). The main body of Paul's letter typically takes up doctrine (1:11—4:31) and specific directions on Christian living (5:1—6:10).

Paul treats each of his opponents' charges in turn. First, he says that he is indeed a legitimate apostle because Jesus appeared to him and called him to witness to him. Later, at the Council of Jerusalem, Paul defended his ministry to the Gentiles, claiming they were free from the Law. The leading apostles agreed:

> When they acknowledged the grace that had been given to me, then James and Cephas [Peter] and John, who were the ones recognized as pillars, offered their right hands to Barnabas and to me as a sign of partnership (Gal 2:9).

Second, Paul defends his teaching about faith and its relationship to salvation. Only faith in the Lord Jesus Christ, not observance of the Jewish Law, guarantees salvation. Faith in Jesus teaches a person to respond to the Spirit, who guides Christians to live holy lives.

Paul also tells the Galatians that baptism incorporates all Christians into God's family. We must act toward each other as brothers and sisters in the Lord:

> For all of you are the children of God, through faith, in Christ Jesus, since every one of you that has been baptized has been clothed in Christ. There can be neither Jew nor Greek, there can be neither slave nor freeman, there can be neither male nor female — for you are all one in Christ Jesus (Gal 3:26–28).

## Exhortation

Chapters 5 and 6 of Galatians outline practical advice on Christian living. Read these two chapters and answer the questions below in your journal.

1. For faith to be effective to what must it be united (5:1–6)?
2. According to Paul, to what does self-indulgence lead (5:13–26)?
3. What are the fruits of the Spirit (5:22–23)? Give examples of how five of these qualities show up in your own life.
4. What is the relationship between our deeds and our destiny (6:1–10)?

**discuss**

1. **What is the difference between true freedom and license?**
2. **Can Christians do whatever they want? What is the test that one is exercising freedom in a Christian, responsible way? Give examples.**

*1 Corinthians.* Corinth was a seaport and prosperous trading center in Greece. It was a Roman colony, with a reputation for permitting every imaginable vice. The expression "living like the Corinthians" meant that a person was very immoral. Paul spent eighteen months there during his second missionary journey, founding and nurturing a Christian community.

When Paul was in Ephesus during his third journey, he received the bad news that the church in Corinth had broken into factions under different leaders. Many members had

also fallen back into immoral pagan practices. So Paul wrote a letter (referred to in 1 Cor 5:11) to warn them away from immorality. This letter is now lost to us. When Paul received further news of division and challenges to his authority, he wrote still another letter, 1 Corinthians, around 54. This down-to-earth, hard-hitting letter took up many practical concerns of the Corinthians and offered good advice for Christians then and now.

1 Corinthians has an opening formula (1:1–3) and a prayer of thanksgiving (1:4–9). The conclusion instructs his readers to take up a collection for the needy and his usual personal greetings (16:1–24). The body of the letter takes up the following themes:

1. *Divisions in the Corinthian community (1:10—4:21).* Four factions emerged in the Corinthian community. Some claimed to be followers of Paul, others of the preacher Apollos, still others of Cephas (Peter). Finally, some boasted that they belonged to Christ and felt they could contact him in a direct religious experience similar to the practices of pagan religions. Paul's answer to all of these groups was simple — rely on the crucified Christ alone: "The message of the cross is folly for those who are on the way to ruin, but for those of us who are on the road to salvation it is the power of God" (1 Cor 1:18).

2. *Problems in Christian morality and living (5:1—11:1).* Paul addressed practical issues such as legal disputes among Christians, sexual immorality, advice on marriage and divorce, and dietary laws. A central topic of concern was the permissiveness that had invaded the Corinthian community. Paul teaches that true Christian freedom is not license to do whatever one wants, but freedom to serve God.

> Do you not realize that your body is the temple of the Holy Spirit, who is in you and whom you received from God? You are not your own property, then; you have been bought at a price. So use your body for the glory of God (1 Cor 6:19–20).

3. *Problems in Christian worship (11:2—14:40).* The divisions in the Corinthian church even spilled over into the way eucharist was celebrated. Selfishness, drunkenness, and quarrels have no place in the meal that celebrates the Lord and Christian unity. Paul teaches that we are all members of Christ's body and that everything must be done in love. The Lord calls us to unity.

4. *Beliefs about the resurrection (15:1–58).* In this section, Paul clarifies proper Christian teaching on the resurrection. He also gives us the earliest Christian creed about Jesus' resurrection (15:3–8).

---

## Reading 1 Corinthians

Read 1 Corinthians 12—15 and record answers to the following questions in your journal.

1. What are the gifts Paul lists in his famous "Body of Christ" passage in Chapter 12?
2. Study Paul's hymn on love (Chapter 13). Give examples of each trait he lists in vv. 4–7.
3. Study Chapter 15. What is the result for us if Christ has *not* risen from the dead? In your own words, explain Paul's image of what our resurrected bodies will be like (15:35ff.).

---

*2 Corinthians.* Between the writing of 1 and 2 Corinthians, Paul returned to Corinth for a short visit to see for himself what was happening there. Apparently neither his letter nor visit had much impact, so Paul wrote another letter, harshly critical of Corinthian abuses. Some scholars believe this letter appears as chapters 10–13 of 2 Corinthians. The major problem Paul addressed was false teachers, probably Judaizers, who had influenced the Corinthians to adopt Jewish laws and customs against the teaching of Paul.

Paul then left Ephesus for Macedonia. While there, he met up with Titus, who told him the Corinthians were beginning to follow Paul's teachings. The Corinthians also asked Paul to visit them again. In response to this happy turn of events and his anticipated visit, Paul wrote 2 Corinthians from somewhere in Macedonia, perhaps in the year 55. Scholars note that this letter seems to be a composite of several others. However, the first nine chapters are much more cheerful and positive in tone as Paul tries to make peace with the Corinthians.

## ▪ *journal* ▪

Read 2 Corinthians 10:1—13:10 and answer the following questions.

1. What accusation is made about Paul as a preacher and letter-writer (10:10–11)? How does Paul defend himself?
2. Why does Paul believe he is equal to any other preacher (chapter 11)?
3. Describe several things Paul reveals about himself and his love for the Corinthians in 12:1—13:10.

*Romans.* Paul, who had not yet visited Rome, wrote this letter to the Christian community there to introduce himself. He was planning to stop in Rome on his way to Spain from Jerusalem and probably wrote to the Romans from Corinth in the winter of 57–58.

Romans is the longest and most theologically developed of all Paul's letters. It treats fully the themes he introduced in Galatians. It also addresses some of the attacks against him that false teachers raised in Corinth. Its central theme is that faith in Jesus saves us and frees us from the Law. However, freedom from the Law does not mean license to do whatever we want. Christian freedom must show itself in Christian service.

The major sections of the letter to the Romans include the following topics:

1. *The human condition before Christ (1:18—3:20).* Paul shows that sin pervades human history. The Gentiles, using their human reason, should have discovered God. However, they worshipped creation instead of the Creator (1:18—2:16). The Jews should have been better off because they had the Law, but they did not keep it. Both Jews and Gentiles are under the power of sin. Apart from Christ Jesus no one can escape God's condemnation (2:17—3:20).

2. *Justification through faith in Christ (3:21—5:21).* Neither the knowledge of the Greeks nor the Jewish Law brings salvation. Only God's gift of grace saves. Jesus' death brings salvation to both Jew and Gentile. "So it is proof of God's own love for us, that Christ died for us while we were still sinners" (Rom 5:8).

3. *Salvation and Christian freedom (6:1—8:39).* Faith in

Christ and baptism accomplish what the Law cannot do for us: freedom from slavery to sin, freedom from the Law, and freedom from death. The Holy Spirit accomplishes this by adopting us into God's family, enabling us to cry, "*Abba*, 'Father!'" (8:15). Our new life in Christ unites us in God's love.

> No; we come through all these things triumphantly victorious, by the power of him who loved us. For I am certain of this: neither death nor life, nor angels, nor principalities, nothing already in existence and nothing still to come, nor any power, nor the heights nor the depths, nor any created thing whatever, will be able to come between us and the love of God, known to us in Christ Jesus our Lord (8:37–39).

4. *God's plan for Israel (9:1—11:36).* These chapters take up Paul's concern for how God's Chosen People fit into this new plan of salvation. Paul points out that God does not contradict his promises to the Jewish people. God's apparent rejection of Israel in offering salvation to the Gentiles is not final. Paul assures his readers that God still loves the Jews, and Paul hopes and prays that they will turn to the gospel.

5. *Christian behavior (12:1—15:13).* Christian faith must translate into concrete deeds of service. Paul sums up Christian responsibility: "Love can cause no harm to your neighbor, and so love is the fulfillment of the Law" (13:10).

## ▪ journal ▪

Read chapters 6—8 of Romans and answer these questions in your journal.

1. What should free us from sin?
2. Why does freedom from the Law not allow us the freedom to sin?
3. Romans 7:14–25 discusses the human struggle to do right.
   a. Who is the only one that can rescue us from the conflict taking place within us?
   b. List several examples in your own life of this quote: "I do not understand my own behavior; I do not act as I mean to, but I do things that I hate" (Rom 7:15).
4. Paul writes: "We are well aware that God works with those who love him, those who have been called in accor-

dance with his purpose, and turns everything to their good" (Rom 8:28). What are your fondest dreams for your future? How might this quote of Paul help you realize them?

5. Discuss some signs that a person is living the life of the Spirit.

*Philippians.* Philippians, with Philemon, Colossians, and Ephesians, is often referred to as a "captivity letter." The traditional view is that it was written while Paul was a prisoner in Rome between 61 and 63. Many scholars, however, believe Philippians may have been written earlier, perhaps during Paul's imprisonment in Caesarea on his way to Rome in 58, or more likely, from Ephesus in 57 or 58.

Paul's love for the Philippians shines through his letter to them. Acts 16:9–40 tells us that Paul established at Philippi the first Christian community in Europe during his second missionary journey in 50. The Philippians were kind to Paul, often sending him financial support. Paul probably visited them two more times, during his third journey on the way to Ephesus (57) and on his way to Jerusalem (58).

The epistle to the Philippians is likely a composite of three short letters Paul sent to this community. A key reason Paul wrote them was to thank them for their financial support (4:14–18) which they sent to him through Epaphroditus who had fallen ill while serving Paul (2:25–30).

Joy in the Lord who lives in the Christian community is a major theme of Philippians. Paul also writes of the need for Christian harmony, peace, and humility, and the necessity to imitate Christ in his sufferings.

## ▪ journal ▪

Read Philippians and answer the following questions.

1. What is Paul's attitude toward death (1:20–26)?
2. The heart of this letter is Paul's quotation of a hymn about Christ, Phil 2:6–11. What is this hymn saying? Give a real example of how you can imitate Christ in his humility.
3. In the third chapter, Paul warns against his enemies in Philippi (3:2–21). Most likely, who were they?
4. Note two verses in chapter 4 in which Paul stresses the theme of joy.

*Philemon.* Philemon is the shortest and most personal of all Paul's letters. Paul wrote to a man named Philemon to encourage him to welcome back with Christian love his runaway slave, Onesimus. Written in Paul's own hand, this letter stresses the dignity owed all Christians who are brothers and sisters in the Lord Jesus.

▪ *journal* ▪

Read Paul's letter to Philemon and answer the following questions in your journal. Discuss your responses in class.

1. What proof does the letter give that Philemon is a Christian?
2. What does Paul reveal about himself in this letter?
3. How does Paul want Philemon to receive Onesimus?
4. What does Paul promise to do concerning any possible harm Onesimus might have caused? How does he try to convince Philemon that his offer is sincere?
5. What verse tells us that Paul hopes to see Philemon again?
6. What does Paul's letter to Philemon tell us about Jesus and his good news?

## Letters Ascribed to Paul

*2 Thessalonians.* Many scholars today believe that disciples of Paul wrote 2 Thessalonians in his name, even slavishly copying some of the same words from 1 Thessalonians.

Some Thessalonians misunderstood or misread what Paul wrote about the resurrection of the dead and Christ's second coming (*parousia*). Some were convinced that Christ was returning very soon, and as a result, they even stopped working while they waited for the Lord. This naturally frustrated the Christians who were working.

> Now we hear that there are some of you who are living lives without any discipline, doing no work themselves but interfering with other people's. In the Lord Jesus Christ, we urge and call on people of this kind to go on quietly working and earning the food that they eat. . . . If anyone refuses to obey what I have written in this

> letter, take note of him and have nothing to do with him, so that he will be ashamed of himself, though you are not to treat him as an enemy, but to correct him as a brother (2 Thes 3:11–12, 14–15).

This advice is loving and fair, but firm. If people refuse to work, then the community can isolate them, not to punish them as much as to encourage them to repent. Our motive for calling the sinner back must always be love for a brother or a sister.

■ *discuss* ■

**How does the attitude and advice in 2 Thes 3:6–15 compare to the church's approach to discipline today?**

*Colossians.* Colossae was a textile town east of Ephesus. Scholars believe that the letter to the Colossians was written sometime shortly after Paul's death, between 70 and 80, by someone who knew Paul's work well. It was written to assist a certain Epaphas, the founder of the Christian community there, in counteracting false teachers. They were spreading ideas about the existence of many different spirits, claiming they intervened in human affairs. Belief in intermediate spirits and practices to appease them wooed the Colossians away from belief in the unique saving role of Christ.

After a typical Pauline address, the author insists that Christ is the pre-eminent spiritual being; he alone can save. Christians should not engage in disciplinary practices regarding food or drink to placate false spirits. The mark of a true Christian is to turn from sin to a life of imitating Jesus in loving others.

The following key verses from Colossians are probably taken from an early Christian hymn to underscore the superiority of Jesus Christ.

> He is the image of the unseen God,
> the first-born of all creation,
> for in him were created all things
> in heaven and on earth:...
> He exists before all things
> and in him all things hold together,
> and he is the Head of the Body,
> that is, the Church.
>
> He is the Beginning,
> the first-born from the dead,
> so that he should be supreme in every way;
> because God wanted all fullness to be found in him

and through him to reconcile all things to him,
everything in heaven and everything on earth,
by making peace through his death on the cross (Col 1:15–20).

*Ephesians.* Many modern scholars believe that Ephesians could be the work of a secretary of Paul or a later disciple, written after Colossians, probably in Ephesus between 80 and 100. The letter draws out more explicitly some of the themes touched on in Colossians. It expands on the image of the church as the Body of Christ first developed by Paul in 1 Corinthians 12. Ephesians further develops this image (1:15–23) and adds to it the image of the church as the Bride of Christ (5:24–33). Ephesians' impersonal tone suggests that it may have originally been a circular letter, meant to be read at many different churches in Asia Minor.

After a short address and greeting, the body of the letter has two main divisions: the mystery of salvation and the church (1:3—3:21) and an exhortation to Christian living in unity (4:1—6:20). The letter ends with the author entrusting the letter to his friend Tychicus, a worthy helper who also delivered the letter to the Colossians.

### ▪ journal ▪

Read Ephesians and answer the following questions.

1. How has God shown his mercy to us (2:1–10)?
2. How should Christians respond to their vocation (4:1–6)?
3. Name four types of behavior redeemed Christians should avoid (4:25—5:5).
4. What images does Paul use in 6:13–17?

*1 and 2 Timothy and Titus.* These three letters were probably the work of the same author, a later follower of Paul who wrote around the year 100. Their style and vocabulary are different from that of Paul, and they reflect a more developed community organization than was present at the time of Paul.

These three letters have the name "pastoral letters" because they were written by one pastor (shepherd) to two other pastors, Timothy and Titus. They differ from Paul's other letters in that they are addressed to individuals and give advice on Christian leadership. Both Timothy and Titus were fellow missionaries with Paul and his faithful disciples. Each of them also shepherded his own Christian community, Timothy in Ephesus and Titus in Crete.

These letters warn against false teachings and teachers and give many practical instructions for church organization and list criteria for church leaders. They also give instructions for Christian worship. Note Paul's advice on the choosing of overseers for the community. This office eventually evolved into the office of bishop.

Finally, these pastoral letters, like all of the Pauline letters, give instructions on Christian living. Family relationships, life within the Christian community, and attitudes toward the government should all reflect the gentleness and love of Christ. Good Christian behavior will attract others to the good news.

▪ *journal* ▪

**Read 1 Timothy and write five specific pieces of advice this letter gives. Discuss whether this advice is still applicable for today's church. Give reasons for your answers.**

## Conclusion

We can only wonder what the history of Christianity would be if the Lord had not appeared to Saul of Tarsus on the road to Damascus. This startling event converted Saul the Pharisee into Paul the missionary to the Gentiles. Acts tells us of his courageous efforts for the Lord. His letters reveal an agile, brilliant mind deeply concerned that his converts not abandon the true Christ.

And who was Jesus Christ for Paul of Tarsus? None other than the crucified Lord who now reigns in glory. Jesus is the Lord of history, the creator of the world, the first fruits of the resurrection, the unique Son of the merciful Father. Jesus is also the head of his body, the church, to which all Christians belong through the power of the Holy Spirit. Our greatest glory in this life is to allow Jesus to live in us. Paul is our model. His life can be summed up in this simple statement: "Life to me ... is Christ (Phil 1:21).

### ▪ *focus questions* ▪

1. Give five significant biographical details of St. Paul's life.
2. What is the earliest Pauline letter? What was a major problem that Paul addressed in this letter?

3. Which of the thirteen letters ascribed to Paul may have been written by his close disciples?
4. Organize any letter of Paul according to the four-fold outline typical of Paul's letters.
5. Discuss five major themes Paul addresses in his letters. Find a passage in Paul's letters to illustrate each theme.
6. Who were the *Judaizers* and what did they teach? What did Paul say to the Galatians to counteract their teachings?
7. According to Paul's teaching, what is the relationship between faith and salvation? Does faith in Jesus absolve us from the Law? Explain.
8. What are the fruits of the Holy Spirit (Gal 5:22–23)?
9. List three problems Paul addressed in 1 Corinthians. What did he teach about each?
10. Discuss five qualities of love Paul lists in his famous hymn on love (1 Cor 13).
11. According to the letter to the Romans, who is under the power of sin? What is the only answer to this dilemma?
12. What is the principle of unity among Christians?
13. Has God rejected the Chosen People? Explain.
14. Why did Paul have special affection for the Philippians?
15. What does 2 Thessalonians teach about Christ's second coming?
16. Which of the Pauline epistles has the most developed theology about the church?
17. Why did Paul write Philemon?
18. What are the three pastoral letters and how did they get their name? Discuss several of the qualities these letters say a good church leader should have.

## ▪ vocabulary ▪

**Copy the meaning of these words into your journal.**

exhortation

placate

vigilant

woo

## ▪ exercises ▪

1. Locate the most difficult verses you read in your study of Paul. Consult a commentary such as the *New Jerome Biblical Commentary* to find out what these verses mean.
2. In the style of a Pauline letter, write a three-hundred-word letter to encourage a classmate who is making a youth retreat.

## Prayer Reflection

Paul quotes several early Christian hymns in his writings. This is the most famous of them. It is worth meditating on.

> Make your own the mind of Christ Jesus:
> Who, being in the form of God,
> did not count equality with God
> something to be grasped.
> But he emptied himself,
> taking the form of a slave,
> becoming as human beings are;
> and being in every way like a human being,
> he was humbler yet,
> even to accepting death, death on a cross.
>
> And for this God raised him high,
> and gave him the name
> which is above all other names;
>
> so that *all beings*
> in the heavens, on earth and in the underworld,
> *should bend the knee* at the name of Jesus
>
> and that *every tongue should acknowledge*
> Jesus Christ as Lord,
> to the glory of God the Father.
>
> — Philippians 2:5–11

### ▪ reflection ▪

Do you truly acknowledge Jesus Christ as Lord? Is he #1 in your life? If not, why not?

### ▪ resolution ▪

Do something for another person in the name of Jesus. Do it out of love for the Lord who gave you eternal life.

*chapter* 10

# Other New Testament Writings

How does it help, my brothers, when someone who has never done a single good act claims to have faith? Will that bring salvation?...But someone may say: So you have faith and I have good deeds? Show me this faith of yours without deeds, then! It is by my deeds that I will show you my faith.

— James 2:14, 18

**In This Chapter**

We will look briefly at:

- Hebrews
- The "catholic" epistles
  - James
  - 1 Peter
  - 1, 2, and 3 John
  - Jude and 2 Peter
- Revelation

An old Irishman once operated a small rowboat to transport passengers across a river. On one oar he had carved the word *Faith* and on the other *Works*. One day a passenger asked the old man the meaning of this. The old man said, "I will show you."

He dropped an oar and began pulling with the one marked *Faith*. Then he did the same with the oar marked *Works*. Both times the boat just went in circles. After this exhibit the clever Irishman picked up both oars and smoothly glided across the water. He explained to his curious passenger: "You see, it is just like this in the Christian life. Works without faith get you nowhere. And faith without works also keeps you from progressing. But faith and works together help you on your way in this life and bring you to eternal destiny in the next."

This story illustrates a major theme of the letter of James, one of the final works in the New Testament. Unless we put our faith in the Lord into practice it is empty. We can apply the same message to our reading of the New Testament. Unless we read our Bibles prayerfully and act on the messages we find there, God's word won't have much effect in transforming our lives.

## Growing in the Christian Life

The New Testament letters contain many teachings on how to grow in the Christian life. Below are six timeless teachings. Examine yourself on each of these teachings using the following scale.

**A** — always
**S** — sometimes
**R** — rarely
**N** — never

____ 1. *"Consider it a great joy when trials of many kinds come upon you, for you well know that the testing of your faith produces perseverance" (Jas 1:2).* Do you look on challenges as opportunities for growth rather than stumbling blocks?

____ 2. *"Do not slander one another" (Jas 4:11).* Are you careful about other people's reputations?

____ 3. *"Any one of you who is in trouble should pray" (Jas 5:13).* Do you turn to the Lord for help when things get tough?

____ 4. *"Humility toward one another must be the garment you all wear constantly" (1 Pt 5:5).* Do you have a proper opinion of yourself, appreciating your essential goodness, but not thinking yourself better than others?

____ 5. *"Support your faith with goodness" (2 Pt 1:5).* Do you make an effort to be an upright person in all you do?

____ 6. *"Let us love each other, since love is from God" (1 Jn 4:7).* Would others say that you are a loving person?

■ *discuss* ■

**What three rules do you think are most essential for living the Christian life?**

■ *journal* ■

Read 2 Peter 1:3–11. Reflect on verses 5–7. Discuss some ways you can exhibit in your own life the qualities mentioned there (faith, goodness, understanding, self-control, perseverance, devotion, kindness, and love).

## Hebrews

Scholars cannot agree on the author or date of Hebrews. Paul did not write it, although for centuries Christians referred to it as Paul's letter to the Hebrews. The style, vocabulary, structure, and use of quotes from the Hebrew scriptures are all different from Paul's letters. The *New Jerome*

*Biblical Commentary* suggests that the author was probably a Gentile Christian who was writing to Jewish Christians in the 60s or 80s to encourage them not to abandon the Christian faith.

Hebrews is a written homily, although the ending is that of a letter. The main theme is the priesthood and sacrifice of Jesus. The author encourages his readers, whose faith in Christ is weakening, to imitate Jesus.

■ *journal* ■

1. Transcribe Hebrews' description of faith (Hb 11:1) into your journal. Write your own definition of faith.
2. Read chapter 7 of Hebrews on Jesus as the high priest. Use the footnotes in your Bible or a biblical dictionary to identify Melchizedek.
3. A priest is a go-between, a mediator between God and humans. List one significant way Jesus is different from all other priests.

## The "Catholic" Epistles

The last seven letters in the New Testament are collectively known as the "catholic letters." The root meaning of *catholic* is "universal." These letters are all addressed to the universal church and not to particular individuals or Christian communities.

*James.* The James designated as the author of this letter was probably the "brother of the Lord," that is, Jesus' relative who was a leader in the early church in Jerusalem. The Jewish historian Josephus tells us that the Jews stoned this James to death in the year 62.

No one can say with absolute certainty who wrote the letter of James or when it was written. The views of James of Jerusalem may have been updated and published by a later Christian teacher sometime in the 90s. Or a Christian teacher versed in both Greek and Jewish thought may have published this letter under the name of James some time in the latter part of the first century.

James is addressed to Jewish Christians who lived outside Palestine. It is more a sermon than a letter. It presents advice and encouragement on themes of Christian morality. It treats many topics: how to handle temptation, how to control one's speech, love of neighbor, the power of prayer, and anointing of the sick. The two main themes throughout the letter are that the rich must care for the poor and that Christian faith must prove itself in action.

## Reading James

Read the letter of James. Then answer these questions in your journal.

1. What image does James use to describe a person who only hears the word of God (1:19ff.)?
2. James says a body without a spirit is dead. What comparison is he making here (2:14–26)?
3. Copy into your journal James' definition of sin, 4:17. Give two examples of sin that he discusses in this chapter.
4. Compare two of the teachings in James 5:1–12 to the teachings of Jesus.
5. According to James, how should the sacrament of the sick take place (5:13ff.)?

### discuss

Read together James 5:16–18.

1. What is the value of confession of sin?
2. James tells us to pray for one another. Do you believe this is a valuable Christian practice? Why or why not? Do you pray for others?

*1 Peter.* The origin of this letter is also uncertain. Perhaps Peter, with the help of his secretary Silvanus (1 Pt 5:12), composed it in the early 60s. Another view is that a later Christian writer, reacting to the widespread persecution of Christians by the emperor Domitian (81–96), wrote it sometime in the 90s.

There is no doubt, however, that 1 Peter was written for pagan converts suffering for their faith. Their acceptance of Jesus and turning from pagan practices brought them ridicule and verbal and physical abuse from their neighbors.

History reveals that Nero (54–68), Domitian, and other emperors persecuted and killed Christians. Jesus' teaching about taking up a cross and following him was not just a pious saying for many early converts. It was reality.

1 Peter contains much practical advice on how newly baptized Christians should remain firm in their faith. The letter has many references to baptism, which reinforces the belief that it was for new converts. Its main themes deal with the dignity of the Christian vocation and suffering for Christ. Throughout, it encourages its readers to stand firm against persecutors.

> Blessed are you if you have to suffer for being upright. *Have no dread of them; have no fear.* Simply *proclaim the Lord* Christ *holy* in your hearts, and always have your answer ready for people who ask you the reason for the hope that you have (3:13–15).
>
> In so far as you share in the sufferings of Christ, be glad, so that you may enjoy a much greater gladness when his glory is revealed. If you are insulted for bearing Christ's name, blessed are you, for *on* you *rests the Spirit of God*, the spirit of glory (4:13–14)

■ *journal* ■

Read 1 Peter 2:11—3:17. Note the advice the author gives to Christian citizens, husbands and wives, and for Christian conduct in general. Does this make sense to you?

*Jude and 2 Peter.* The authorship of these letters is uncertain. Scholars believe Jude was probably written in the 90s. 2 Peter, attributed to Peter but written by a later author, borrows heavily from Jude 4–16. Scholars date it around the year 100 or even later, perhaps the latest New Testament writing. Both letters address Christians who were beginning to distort the true teaching that they received. For example, because the Lord had not yet come back, some Christian teachers were beginning to deny that he ever would. This led some of them to fall back into bad habits, forgetting that the Lord will eventually judge us for our deeds. These letters encourage their readers to remain faithful to true teaching and continue to live the Christian life.

■ *journal* ■

**Read 2 Peter 3:1-18 and answer these questions.**

1. **What rules the scoffers (v. 3)?**
2. **How does the author explain the apparent delay of the Lord?**
3. **How should we live until the day the Lord comes?**

*1, 2, and 3 John.* These three letters are so similar in style and teaching that most scholars conclude that they are closely related to John's gospel. They were probably written after it, perhaps in the late 90s or the year 100. By far, the most important of the three letters is 1 John, written to bolster communities threatened by false teaching.

There is a sense of urgency in this letter because gnostics had infiltrated the churches to which the letter was sent. These false teachers claimed special knowledge (in the Greek, *gnosis*) about Jesus and the Christian life, knowledge they said came from mystical experiences with Christ. These people acted superior to their fellow Christians, thought the physical world was evil, and held that Jesus was only a spiritual being who came to teach a select few the secrets of eternal life.

The particular brand of gnosticism that infected the communities for whom John wrote was *docetism*. This heresy held that Jesus only seemed to be human (from the Greek word *dokeo*, "to seem"). In effect, the docetists denied the Incarnation of Jesus. Because they thought material reality was perverse, they could not imagine how God could become human. Docetism is a dangerous heresy with immense consequences. If Jesus was not truly a human being, then he did not really die for us nor did he rise from the dead. If this is so, then Jesus could not really be the savior of the world.

1 John relentlessly attacks these views throughout the letter. Christians must have true belief in Jesus, and these beliefs should manifest themselves in love for others. According to 1 John, a person cannot call himself or herself a Christian unless he or she imitates the love of Christ for all people.

■ *journal* ■

**Read 1 John and briefly state a key point from each chapter of this letter. Give references to the letter itself.**

God's true revelation is Jesus Christ. He is truly the Son of God and Messiah whose blood cleanses us from sin. If we wish to be children of the light, then we must turn from sin and live upright lives. The antichrist is anyone who denies that Jesus is the Messiah. The true Christian must imitate Jesus and follow the commandments, particularly Jesus' greatest commandment to love one another.

## Revelation

*Why Was Revelation Written?* Picture yourself as a Christian living somewhere in the Roman Empire in the last decade of the first century. It was dangerous to be a Christian. The reigning emperor, Domitian (A.D. 81–96), insisted that his subjects take part in emperor worship. He required people to burn incense on an altar built to him and proclaim his divinity: "Caesar is Lord." The penalty for refusal was death.

Faithful Christians would never worship a false god like the emperor and thus deny their faith in the unique divinity of God's own Son, Jesus Christ. Many lost their lives witnessing to Jesus. However, under the threat of death, some Christians gave up their faith, and many others were wavering.

The author of Revelation, a prophet named John, knew the danger of being a Christian firsthand. He was exiled to the island of Patmos because of his preaching of the gospel. The author was likely a disciple of John the apostle, probably from the same Ephesus community that produced the gospel and the letters named after John.

The author of Revelation begins this way:

> A revelation of Jesus Christ, which God gave him so that he could tell his servants *what is now to take place* very soon; he sent his angel to make it known to his servant John, and John has borne witness to the Word of God and to the witness of Jesus Christ, everything that he saw. Blessed is anyone who reads the words of this prophecy, and blessed those who hear them, if they treasure the content, because the Time is near (Rv 1:1–3).

Revelation (*Apocalypse* in Greek), means "unveiling." The prophet John claims that the Lord Jesus sent him visions to unveil what is going to take place in the future. This is where the book of Revelation gets its name. Behind all the symbolism and strange visions, John has a simple message for his readers: Although you are suffering now, endure. The Lamb of God has triumphed! Victory is ours! Persevere. "I am indeed coming soon" (Rv 22:20).

*Why So Much Symbolism?* The book of Revelation is the last book in the Bible. It is perhaps the least read and most misunderstood, primarily because it is so highly symbolic. While it contains several types of biblical literature, the dominant literary form is apocalyptic writing, which was popular in Jewish circles between 200 B.C. and A.D. 200. The book of Daniel (especially Dn 7—12) is an excellent example of an apocalypse from the Hebrew scriptures.

The basic message of apocalyptic writing is that God controls history and the outcome of events, not the present evil rulers or the forces of evil. God will usher in a golden age of peace and justice. The glorious outcome is God's pure gift; nothing we do can bring it about. In the meantime, we should patiently endure suffering and live a Christian life.

However, apocalyptic writing couches this simple message in a style that is both highly symbolic and weirdly imaginative, talking about multi-headed dragons and beasts, a Christ-figure with seven horns and seven eyes, and trumpets blasting out plagues on humanity. An ancient scholar said that studying the book of Revelation either finds us crazy or makes us crazy. St. Jerome commented that it contains as many secrets as it does words.

We must assume that Revelation's original audience knew the meaning of most of the references. Scholars today have figured out many of them. The prophet may very well have disguised his message in symbols so he could write about his enemies without naming them, in case the book fell into their hands. In this time of persecution everything connected with Christianity was suspect.

Here are a few of the symbols Revelation uses.

Numbers:

*7* means wholeness or perfection.

*6*, one short of 7, means imperfection.

*3–1/2* is half of seven and thus also represents imperfection.

*12* signifies Israel or the 12 apostles.

*1000* symbolizes an incalculable amount or eternity. (12 x 12 x 1000 equals 144,000, which is a symbol of the new Israel that embraces every nation, race, people, and language.)

*4* represents the whole world (the four corners of the earth).

Colors:

*Black* represents death, unfaithfulness, evil.

*Red* means violence, killing, the blood of witnesses.

*White* symbolizes purity and victory.

Names and Figures:

*Babylon*, an ancient city that persecuted the Jews, stands for the modern persecutor of the Christians, *Rome*. She is a *harlot* and anyone who worships the emperor is a *fornicator* or *adulterer*. Nero and Domitian, both of whom persecuted Christians, are *beasts*.

A *dragon* represents evil.

*Four horses* of the Apocalypse: the *white* horse symbolizes conquering power, the *red* horse signifies bloody war, the *black* horse means famine, and the *green* horse represents death.

A *horn* symbolizes power while *eyes* symbolize knowledge. Describing Jesus as having seven eyes and seven horns is a symbolic way of saying he is all-powerful and all-knowing.

**The most famous number in Revelation is 666. This number represents the ultimate imperfection or evil because it falls short of the number 7 (perfection) three times. Many scholars identify 666 with the emperor Nero who first persecuted the Christians. In the Greek and Hebrew languages, each letter has a numerical value. In Hebrew letters, the name Caesar Nero adds up to 666.**

*How Should We Interpret Revelation Today?* Do these symbols refer to people and events in our world today? Does knowledge of their meaning tell you when the world is going to end? Some Christians elevate the book of Revelation to a place of supreme importance among all the New Testament books. They believe the book has hidden meaning about God's ultimate plans for us, even down to the very day when our present world will end. Some fundamentalist preachers fill the airwaves with predictions of a great cosmic clash waiting just around the corner.

The Catholic interpretation is that the author of the book of Revelation wrote primarily to encourage *his* contemporaries. Our first task is to see what he was saying to them. Also, the basic message of Revelation has universal application. Even in our own day, we need hopeful reminders of the Lord's control of history, that good will triumph over evil. We also need encouragement to remain faithful to Jesus in times of crisis, temptation, and suffering.

However, the book of Revelation was not written so we can look to the latest earthquake, dictator, or war as the definitive sign of Christ's second coming. People who speculate on the exact time of the world's end ignore Jesus' teaching (Mk 13:32) to leave this in God's hands. We should be concerned about living each day in a committed, loving, serving way.

Christians look to the future with hope. But we also believe we can meet the Lord in the eucharist, in his scriptural word, in the depths of our own hearts, and in the people he sends into our lives. When we pray "Come, Lord Jesus" (Rv 22:20), we also know that he is already here.

▪ *journal* ▪

Read Revelation 21—22. These last chapters beautifully describe the heavenly city that awaits all Christians who endure suffering in this life. Their constant prayer — "Come, Lord Jesus" — is answered now and will be answered always.

1. Why is there no need for a temple in the new city?
2. What is your own image of heaven? Compare it to Revelation's poetic image.

## Conclusion

As we conclude our study of the New Testament, let's look back on what we have accomplished. In reading a substantial part of the New Testament, we have learned how it came into existence, studied its major themes, and seen how scholars approach it. Furthermore, we have seen how it preserves, conveys, and brings to life the good news of the gospel of Jesus Christ.

Thank you for the effort you put into your study. As you continue on your faith journey, frequently return to the Bible to experience again and again the truths that bring us eternal life. The book of Revelation ends with a beautiful prayer (22:21). It is a fitting petition with which to end this book.

"May the grace of the Lord Jesus be with you all. Amen."

## focus questions

1. What is the main theme of the letter to the Hebrews?
2. What are the seven "catholic" epistles and how did they get their name?
3. How does the letter of James understand the relationship between faith and works? Give several examples.
4. For whom was 1 Peter written?
5. What is the relationship between Jude and 2 Peter?
6. According to 2 John, who is the antichrist?
7. Identify the term *docetism*. What other *gnostic* teachings were associated with the communities of the author of 1 John?
8. What does 1 John say about love?
9. Should we look to the book of Revelation for answers about the end of the world? Why or why not?
10. Who wrote Revelation and why? Why does the book contain so much symbolism?
11. What is apocalyptic writing? What purpose does it serve?
12. What is the theme of the book of Revelation?
13. Discuss the meaning of any ten symbols in the book of Revelation.

## vocabulary

**Copy the meaning of these words into your journal:**

**apocalyptic**

**scoffer**

## exercise

Do one of the following:

a. If you have artistic talent, try your hand at drawing any of the symbols or creatures mentioned in the book of Revelation.

b. Construct an outline for a ten-minute talk on the New Testament. Pick out your five favorite passages and list points about their meaning and application to the daily life of a teen.

c. Write your own description of the end of the world, judgment, and heaven. Let your imagination run wild.

---

## Prayer Reflection

Put yourself in the presence of the Lord by studying a crucifix. Slowly and carefully read these words from Hebrews:

> Let us keep our eyes fixed on Jesus, who leads us in our faith and brings it to perfection: for the sake of the joy which lay ahead of him, he endured the cross, disregarding the shame of it, and *has taken his seat at the right* of God's throne. Think of the way he persevered against such opposition from sinners and then you will not lose heart and come to grief.
>
> — Hebrews 12:2–3

### ■ reflection ■

What do you see when you look at the cross of Christ? What does Jesus see when he looks back into your eyes?

### ■ resolution ■

What major obstacle do you face in your life right now? Ask the Lord to help you persevere.

---

# Glossary of Selected Terms

*Apocalypse* — A Greek word for "revelation." It also refers to a type of highly symbolic literature that discusses the future and the final judgment. This form of literature was used to give hope to a persecuted people that God's goodness will triumph over evil.

*Apostle* — One who is sent by Jesus to continue his work.

*Biblical criticism* — This method of the study of biblical texts tries to discover what the particular passage or book meant to its original audience. It uses form, historical, source, and redaction criticism.

*Canon (of the Bible)* — The official list of the inspired books of the Bible. Catholics list forty-six books from the Hebrew scriptures and twenty-seven New Testament books.

*Catechesis* — The process of religious instruction and formation in the major elements of the Christian faith.

*Concordance* — A book or computer program that contains all the words of the Bible giving their citation by book, chapter, and verse.

*Covenant* — The open-ended contract of love God made first with the Israelites and then with all people everywhere in the person of Jesus Christ.

*Disciple* — A follower of Jesus. Christians are disciples who try to model their life on Jesus.

*Epistle* — A New Testament letter usually intended for public reading. Most epistles have these elements: (1) an opening address; (2) a thanksgiving; (3) the body of the letter with doctrinal teaching and a section of encouragement; and (4) final salutations.

*Evangelist* — A person who proclaims the good news of Jesus Christ. "The four evangelists" refers to the authors of the four gospels: Matthew, Mark, Luke, and John.

*Form criticism* — A method of studying biblical texts by focusing on the smaller literary units in a work, for example, a parable. The method tries to discover how the smaller unit originated in the period of oral tradition before it appeared as part of the larger written work.

*Gospel* — Literally, "good news." Gospel refers to (1) the good news preached by Jesus; (2) the good news of salvation won for us in the person of Jesus Christ (he is the good news proclaimed by the church); (3) the four written records of the good news — the gospels of Matthew, Mark, Luke, and John.

*Gnosticism* — A philosophy derived from the Greek word *gnosis* which means knowledge. It claimed secret knowledge about the nature of spiritual realities. Gnostics generally distrusted material creation. One form of gnosticism — docetism — denied that Jesus was ever really a man.

*Historical criticism* — Studies the Bible (including its traditions) as a historical document. Its basic question is: "What really happened?" Different methods of historical research are used to ascertain the historical basis of a biblical narrative in so far as this is possible.

*Incarnation* — A key theological term for the dogma of the Son of God becoming human in Jesus Christ, born of the Virgin Mary. (The term literally means "taking on human flesh.")

*Inspiration (of the Bible)* — The guidance of the Holy Spirit that enabled the biblical writers to record what God wanted revealed.

*Kerygma* — The core or essential message and preaching of the gospel. An excellent example of the kerygma is found in Acts 2:14–36.

*Liturgy* — The official public worship of the church. The seven sacraments, especially the eucharist, are the primary forms of liturgical celebration.

*Magisterium* — The teaching authority of the church. The Lord bestowed the right to teach in his name on the apostles and their successors, that is, the bishops and pope as their leader.

*Parable* — A short story told by Jesus with a striking, memorable comparison that teaches a religious message.

*Parousia* — The second coming of Christ, which will usher in the full establishment of God's reign on earth as it is in heaven.

*Paschal mystery* — God's love and salvation revealed to us through the life, passion, death, resurrection, and glorification of Jesus Christ.

*Passover* — The most important Jewish feast which celebrates the exodus, Yahweh's deliverance of the Chosen People from Egypt.

*Pentecost* — The feast which commemorates the descent of the Holy Spirit upon the apostles and the beginning of their preaching of the gospel. It is sometimes called the "birthday of the church." The Jewish feast of Pentecost, a harvest festival, occurred fifty days after Passover and celebrated Yahweh's giving of the Law to Moses.

*Redaction criticism* — A method of studying a biblical text which analyzes how the biblical author edited (redacted) the text from the materials at hand. Often the editor would adapt the text for his particular audience.

*Reign of God* — The reign of God (also called the kingdom of God) was proclaimed by Jesus and inaugurated in his life, death, and resurrection. It refers to the process of God reconciling and renewing all things through his Son, to the fact of his will being done on earth as it is in heaven. The process began with Jesus and will be perfectly completed at the end of time.

*Sanhedrin* — The chief ruling council in Jesus' day made up of the elders, the high priests, and the scribes.

*Septuagint* — An important ancient Greek translation of the Hebrew scriptures. The word *Septuagint* comes from the Latin word for "seventy" referring to the legendary 70 (or 72) scholars who translated the work in 72 days.

*Source criticism* — A way of studying biblical texts that tries to discover the documents that helped the biblical authors construct their own works. Source criticism has discovered, for example, that Matthew and Luke shared *Q* (abbreviation for the German *Quelle*, meaning "source") as one of their sources in writing their gospels.

*Synoptic gospels* — The gospels of Matthew, Mark, and Luke. When "looked at together" (*syn* + *optic* in Greek), we note certain similarities in content and style. Matthew and Luke both borrowed from Mark and a source known as *Q* as well as their own unique materials.

*Torah* — The Law handed down to the Jewish people which they were to live in response to God's covenant with them. A good summary of the Torah is found in the Ten Commandments.

*Vulgate* — St. Jerome's fifth-century translation of the Bible into Latin, the common language of the people of his day.

# Index